THE ILLUSTRATOR'S NOTEBOOK

THE ILLUSTRATOR'S NOTEBOOK

Edited by Lee Kingman

THE HORN BOOK, INCORPORATED

BOSTON · 1978

Printed in the United States of America

Library of Congress Cataloging in Publication Data

The Illustrator's notebook.

Essays originally appeared in The Horn book magazine.
Bibliography: p. 143
Includes index.
1. Illustration of books — Addresses, essays, lectures.
2. Illustrators — Addresses, essays, lectures.
I. Kingman, Lee. II. The Horn book magazine.
NC960.I44   741.64   77-20028

ISBN 0-87675-013-7

Acknowledgments

GRATEFUL ACKNOWLEDGMENT is made to the following authors, artists, agents, and publishers for their kind permission to use text and illustrations:

ADDISON-WESLEY PUBLISHING COMPANY
59. From *Nibble, Nibble,* © 1959, by Margaret Wise Brown. Illustrations Copyright © 1959 by Leonard Weisgard. A Young Scott Book, reprinted by permission of ADDISON-WESLEY PUBLISHING COMPANY, INC.
12. From *Sara and the Door.* Text Copyright © 1977 by Virginia Allen Jensen. Illustrations Copyright © 1977 by Ann Strugnell. Reprinted by permission of ADDISON-WESLEY PUBLISHING COMPANY, INC.
50. From *Two Little Trains,* © 1949 and 1977, by Margaret Wise Brown, illustrated by Jean Charlot. A Young Scott Book, reprinted by permission of ADDISON-WESLEY PUBLISHING COMPANY, INC.

MARCIA BROWN
Excerpts from "My Goals as an Illustrator" © 1967 by Marcia Brown.
26, 29. From *Backbone of the King.* Copyright © 1966 Marcia Brown.

THE CHILDREN'S BOOK COUNCIL
Excerpts from "On Illustrators — My View" by Walter Lorraine reprinted by permission of The Children's Book Council from *The Calendar.*

WILLIAM COLLINS & WORLD PUBLISHING COMPANY
58. From *A Pair of Red Clogs* by Masako Matsuno, illustrated by Kazue Mizamura. Text Copyright © 1960 by Masako Matsuno. Illustrations Copyright © 1960 by Kazue Mizamura. Reprinted by permission of WILLIAM COLLINS & WORLD PUBLISHING COMPANY.
60. From *The Secret Hiding Place* written and illustrated by Rainey Bennett. Copyright © 1960 by Rainey Bennett. Reprinted by permission of WILLIAM COLLINS & WORLD PUBLISHING COMPANY and ABELARD-SCHUMAN LIMITED.

COWARD, MCCANN & GEOGHEGAN, INC.
36. From *Tales from Grimm* by Wanda Gág, Copyright 1936 by Wanda Gág; renewed 1964 by Robert Janssen. Reprinted by permission of COWARD, MCCANN & GEOGHEGAN, INC.

THOMAS Y. CROWELL COMPANY, INC.
49. From *Chanticleer and the Fox* by Geoffrey Chaucer, adapted and illustrated by Barbara Cooney. Illustration Copyright © 1958 by Thomas Y. Crowell Company, Inc. Reprinted by permission of THOMAS Y. CROWELL COMPANY, INC.
90. From *Grandfather Whiskers, M.D.* by Nellie M. Leonard, illustrated by Barbara Cooney. Illustration Copyright © 1953 by Thomas Y. Crowell Company, Inc. Reprinted by permission of THOMAS Y. CROWELL COMPANY, INC.
9. From *Little Women* by Louisa M. Alcott, illustrated by Barbara Cooney. Illustrations Copyright © 1955 by Barbara Cooney. Reprinted by permission of THOMAS Y. CROWELL COMPANY, INC.
64. From *Sir Gawain and the Green Knight* by Constance Hieatt, illustrated by Walter Lorraine. Illustrations Copyright © 1967 by Walter Lorraine. Reprinted by permission of THOMAS Y. CROWELL COMPANY, INC.
40. From *A White Heron* by Sarah Orne Jewett, illustrated by Barbara Cooney. Illustrations Copyright © 1963 by Barbara Cooney. Reprinted by permission of THOMAS Y. CROWELL COMPANY, INC.
93. From *Colonial Craftsmen and the Beginnings of American Industry* written and illustrated by Edwin Tunis. Copyright © 1965 by Edwin Tunis. Reprinted by permission of THOMAS Y. CROWELL COMPANY, INC., and CURTIS BROWN, LTD.
94. From *Frontier Living* written and illustrated by Edwin Tunis. Copyright © 1961. Reprinted by permission of THOMAS Y. CROWELL COMPANY, INC., and CURTIS BROWN, LTD.

ROSE DOBBS
Excerpts from "Wanda Gág, Fellow-Worker" by Rose Dobbs.

DOUBLEDAY & COMPANY, INC.
Quotes from Mary Cassatt by Nancy Hale. Copyright © 1975 by Nancy Hale. Reprinted by permission of DOUBLEDAY & COMPANY, INC., and HAROLD OBER ASSOCIATES.

and Lynd Ward. Reprinted by permission of HOUGHTON MIFFLIN COMPANY.

18. From *Sleepy Ronald* by Jack Gantos, illustrated by Nicole Rubel. Copyright © 1976 by John B. Gantos, Jr. Copyright © 1976 by Leslie Rubel. Reprinted by permission of HOUGHTON MIFFLIN COMPANY.

39. From *Song of Robin Hood*. Selected and edited by Anne Malcolmson, designed and illustrated by Virginia Lee Burton. Copyright, 1947, by Anne Burnett Malcolmson and Virginia Lee Demetrios; copyright renewed 1975. Reprinted by permission of HOUGHTON MIFFLIN COMPANY.

13, 14, 15. From *The Favorite Uncle Remus* by Joel Chandler Harris, selected, arranged, and edited by George Van Santvoord and Archibald C. Coolidge, illustrated by A. B. Frost. Copyright, 1948, by Houghton Mifflin Company. Reprinted by permission of HOUGHTON MIFFLIN COMPANY.

70. From *The Wave* by Margaret Hodges, illustrated by Blair Lent. Copyright © 1964 by Margaret Hodges; Copyright © 1964 by Blair Lent. Reprinted by permission of HOUGHTON MIFFLIN COMPANY and MC INTOSH AND OTIS, INC.

98. From *Why the Sun and the Moon Live in the Sky* by Elphinstone Dayrell, illustrated by Blair Lent. Copyright © 1968 by Blair Lent, Jr. Reprinted by permission of HOUGHTON MIFFLIN COMPANY.

DAHLOV IPCAR
Excerpts from "Making Pictures on the Farm" © 1977 by Dahlov Ipcar.
Excerpts from "Combining Dinobase and Wash on Paper" © 1977 by Dahlov Ipcar.

ALFRED A. KNOPF, INC.
44. From *Black and White* text and illustrations by Dahlov Ipcar. Copyright © 1963 by Dahlov Ipcar. Reprinted by permission of ALFRED A. KNOPF, INC., and MC INTOSH AND OTIS, INC.

86. From *The Calico Jungle*, text and illustrations by Dahlov Ipcar. Copyright © 1965 by Dahlov Ipcar. Reprinted by permission of ALFRED A. KNOPF, INC., and MC INTOSH AND OTIS, INC.

5, 6. From *The Nutcracker*, text and illustrations by Warren Chappell. Copyright © 1958 by Warren Chappell. Reprinted by permission of ALFRED A. KNOPF, INC.

43. From *Ten Big Farms*, text and illustrations by Dahlov Ipcar. Copyright © 1958 by Dahlov Ipcar. Reprinted by permission of ALFRED A. KNOPF, INC., and MC INTOSH AND OTIS, INC.

J. B. LIPPINCOTT COMPANY
45. From *Bertie's Escapade* by Kenneth Grahame, illustrated by Ernest H. Shepard. Illustrations copyright 1949 by Ernest H. Shepard. Reprinted by permission of J. B. LIPPINCOTT COMPANY and CURTIS BROWN LTD.

LITTLE, BROWN AND COMPANY
85. From *Lady Bird, Quickly* by Juliet Kepes. Copyright © 1964 by Juliet Kepes. Reprinted by permission of LITTLE, BROWN AND COMPANY in association with THE ATLANTIC MONTHLY PRESS.

41. From *Le Hibou et la Poussiquette* French text by Francis Steegmuller, pictures by Barbara Cooney. Illustration Copyright © 1961 by Barbara Cooney. Reprinted by permission of LITTLE, BROWN AND COMPANY.

92. From *Punch and Judy: A Play for Puppets* by Ed Emberley. Copyright © 1965 by Edward R. Emberley. Reprinted by permission of LITTLE, BROWN AND COMPANY.

LOTHROP, LEE & SHEPARD COMPANY
55. From *A for the Ark* by Roger Duvoisin. Copyright 1952 by Lothrop, Lee & Shepard Company, Inc. Reprinted by permission of LOTHROP, LEE & SHEPARD COMPANY and THE BODLEY HEAD.

GERALD MC DERMOTT
Excerpts from "On the Rainbow Trail" © 1975 by Gerald McDermott.

THE OVERLOOK PRESS
Quotes from *Milton Glaser: Graphic Design*. © 1973 by Milton Glaser. First published in 1973 by The Overlook Press, Lewis Hollow Road, Woodstock, N. Y. Reprinted by permission of THE OVERLOOK PRESS.

OXFORD UNIVERSITY PRESS
51. From *Tim to the Rescue* by Edward Ardizzone, first published in 1949 by Oxford University Press. Reprinted by permission of OXFORD UNIVERSITY PRESS.

PHILOMENA C. T. PALAZZO
47. From *Susie the Cat* by Tony Palazzo. Copyright 1949 by Tony Palazzo. Reprinted by permission of PHILOMENA C. T. PALAZZO, Executrix, the Estate of Anthony Palazzo.

PANTHEON BOOKS
21. From *Alexander and the Wind-Up Mouse*, text and illustrations by Leo Lionni. Copyright © 1969 by Leo Lionni. Reprinted by permission of PANTHEON BOOKS, a Division of Random House, Inc., and ABELARD-SCHUMAN LIMITED.

CHARLES SCRIBNER'S SONS
69. From *Josefina February* by Evaline Ness.

Copyright © 1963 Evaline Ness. Reprinted by permission of CHARLES SCRIBNER'S SONS.

27. From *Once a Mouse* by Marcia Brown. Copyright © 1961 Marcia Brown. Reprinted by permission of CHARLES SCRIBNER'S SONS.

66. From *Mr. Peaceable Paints* by Leonard Weisgard. Copyright © 1956 Leonard Weisgard. Reprinted by permission of CHARLES SCRIBNER'S SONS.

53. From *The Thanksgiving Story* by Alice Dalgliesh, illustrated by Helen Sewell. Copyright 1954 Alice Dalgliesh and Helen Sewell. Reprinted by permission of CHARLES SCRIBNER'S SONS.

34, 35. From *The Wind in the Willows* by Kenneth Grahame, illustrated by Ernest H. Shepard. Copyright, 1933, 1953 Charles Scribner's Sons. Reprinted by permission of CHARLES SCRIBNER'S SONS.

28. From *The Wild Swans* by Hans Christian Andersen, illustrated by Marcia Brown. Copyright © 1963 Marcia Brown. Reprinted by permission of CHARLES SCRIBNER'S SONS.

URI SHULEVITZ
Excerpts from "Within the Margins of a Picture Book" © 1971 by Uri Shulevitz.

SIMON & SCHUSTER
1. From *Heroes of the Kalevala* by Babette Deutsch, illustrated by Fritz Eichenberg. Copyright © 1940 by Babette Deutsch, renewed © 1967 by Babette Deutsch. Reprinted by permission of SIMON & SCHUSTER, a Division of Gulf and Western Corporation.

UNIVERSITY OF CHICAGO PRESS
Quote reprinted from *Boardman Robinson* by Albert Christ-Janer, Copyright 1946 by The University of Chicago, by permission of THE UNIVERSITY OF CHICAGO PRESS.

THE VIKING PRESS, INC.
100. From *Arrow to the Sun* by Gerald McDermott. Copyright © 1974 by Gerald McDermott. Reproduced by permission of THE VIKING PRESS.
23. From *Bear Circus* by William Pène du Bois. Copyright © 1971 by William Pène du Bois. Reproduced by permission of THE VIKING PRESS. and WORLD'S WORK LTD.
8. From *Canadian Summer* by Hilda van Stockum. Copyright 1948 by Hilda van Stockum Marlin. Reproduced by permission of THE VIKING PRESS.
56. From *Crow Boy* by Taro Yashima. Copyright © 1955 by Mitsu and Taro Yashima. Repro-
duced by permission of THE VIKING PRESS.
19. From *The Crystal Apple* by Beverly Brodsky McDermott. Copyright © 1974 by Beverly Brodsky McDermott. Reproduced by permission of THE VIKING PRESS.
22. From *Hosie's Alphabet* words by Hosea, Tobias and Lisa Baskin, pictures by Leonard Baskin. Copyright © 1972 in all countries of the International Copyright Union by Leonard Baskin. Reproduced by permission of THE VIKING PRESS.
17. From *Moon-Whales and Other Moon Poems* by Ted Hughes, illustrated by Leonard Baskin. Copyright © 1963, 1976 by Ted Hughes. Illustrations Copyright © 1976 by Leonard Baskin. Reproduced by permission of THE VIKING PRESS and OLWYN HUGHES.
46. From *Play With Me* by Marie Hall Ets. Copyright © 1955 by Marie Hall Ets. Reproduced by permission of THE VIKING PRESS.
68. From *Whistle for Willie* by Ezra Jack Keats. Copyright © 1964 by Ezra Jack Keats. Reproduced by permission of THE VIKING PRESS and THE BODLEY HEAD.

HENRY Z. WALCK, INC.
52. From *A Bell for Ursli* by Selina Chönz, illustrated by Alois Carigiet. First published in this edition 1950. Reprinted by permission of HENRY Z. WALCK, INC., a division of David McKay Co., Inc.
2. From *Grimm's Tales* illustrated by Helen Sewell and Madeleine Gekiere. Copyright 1954 Oxford University Press, Inc. Reprinted by permission of HENRY Z. WALCK, INC., a division of David McKay Co., Inc.

LYND WARD
3, 4. From *Gods' Man A Novel in Woodcuts* by Lynd Ward. Copyright 1929 and 1957 by Lynd Ward. Reprinted by permission of Lynd Ward.

THE H. W. WILSON COMPANY
Quotes from *The Child's First Books, A Critical Study of Pictures and Texts* by Donnarae MacCann and Olga Richard. © 1973 by Donnarae MacCann and Olga Richard. Reprinted by permission of THE H. W. WILSON COMPANY, publisher.
25. *The Doryman*, painting by N. C. Wyeth. Copyright © 1938 by N. C. Wyeth. Courtesy of Mrs. Norman B. Woolworth.

We are also grateful to all the authors and artists who allowed us to reprint excerpts from their articles which originally appeared in *The Horn Book Magazine*.

Contents

Introduction

When the body of a book is illustrated with eye-catching pictures and the text is composed of mind-catching material, the temptation to reader and browser alike is to skip hastily past the introduction. So the temptation to the editor is to drop the heading Introduction and boldly announce *Directions: please read before using.*

This book is multi-purpose. It is intended for artists who have little knowledge of the development and history of illustration, particularly in the children's book field; for those with fine arts training but little or no technical or commercial experience; for those with technical or commercial training but little experience with a fine arts approach; and for authors, teachers, students, librarians, and parents who are interested in children's book illustration in general.

As the title implies, the form is often that of notes or excerpts from longer articles — to be referred to just as an illustrator refers to his carefully nurtured clipping file of pictures.

The incipient illustrator has often been rushed through training which may have prepared him in the use of every technique from cardboard cuts to airbrush. But too often his training has left out the rich background found in liberal arts courses and, in particular, has omitted the philosophy and history of children's literature. Or the reverse — the fine artist has been allowed to wallow his way through imaginative and intellectual approaches, encouraged to free his creativity in all kinds of media without consideration of the technical problems of preparing artwork for reproduction.

Most art schools have a history of separation of fine art, or high art, from technical art and/or graphics. Today in some art schools graphics has an even more specific connotation — graphics as the means of visual communication, rather than just as the means of a reproduction process such as etching or lithography.

In the 1940s I had the temerity to take over a course in "The Preparation of Illustration for Mechanical Reproduction" at the Museum School of Fine Art, Boston, which was being taught by Grace Allen Hogarth, then Editor of Children's Books at Houghton Mifflin. When she returned to England during World War II, I inherited both her job at Houghton Mifflin and her teaching stint at the Museum School, unfortunately without her training in fine arts or her experience as an illustrator, although I did manage to keep at least one week ahead of the students. What bothered me most at the time, however, was discovering that the fine arts and the graphics departments not only ignored each other, but that illustration was treated as a rather curious illegitimate child. As I was still learning my own way in the field of children's literature, I could not give to the students the benefit of knowledge accumulated later — that of the importance of such seminal figures as the English artists Caldecott, Brooke, Crane, and Rackham; the French, Boutet de Monvel and Edy Legrand; and the American, A. B. Frost, Howard Pyle, and E. Boyd Smith.

One has only to read *The Brandywine Tradition* by Henry C. Pitz to realize the intensity of purpose and dedication to high standards which made Howard Pyle the artist he was and that led him to encourage, teach, and set standards for others. Pyle also had a unique view — that of the whole artist undivided into illustrator or fine artist.

"... In a letter [written in 1900] to the artist Edward Penfield who was acting as art editor for Harper, [Pyle wrote] ... 'My final aim in teaching will not be essentially the production of illustrators of books, but rather the production of painters of pictures. For I believe that the painters of true American Art are yet to be produced. Such men as Winslow Homer ... in figure painting, and a group of landscape painters headed by George Innes as yet are almost the only occupants of the field. To this end I regard magazine and book illustration as a ground from which to produce painters ... I shall make it a requisite that the pupil whom I choose shall possess first of all, imagination; secondly, artistic ability; thirdly, color and drawing; and I shall probably not accept any who are deficient in any one of these three requisites.' "[1]

Howard Pyle was the first artist to establish such a personal school of teaching, in which he shared his home, his daily life, his studios, and his own work with a selected group of students. It was very different from other training available to art students, especially that described by Thomas Handforth at the École des Beaux Arts in Paris, where the students "did a charcoal drawing of a nude model on a large sheet of paper, beginning at 9 o'clock on Monday morning, with the head at the top of the page and finishing at the bottom of the page with the feet at exactly noon on Saturday."[2] To my knowledge, no one today is conducting any such personal program, as Pyle did, of live-in teaching of art/illustration, with a variety of subjects scheduled to take a period of two to three years or even longer.

The most revealing facet of *The Brandywine Tradition* in its discussion of Pyle, N. C. Wyeth and others, however, is that of the maturation of an illustrator. No one expected overnight success even in the days when illustrators had far more opportunity to sell their work than they do today; there were so many magazines, including the prestigious *Scribner's Magazine* and *Harper's Magazine*, which bought drawings and paintings and gave assignments to artists to illustrate articles and stories. Becoming an artist-illustrator was expected to take years of faithful hard apprenticeship. Drawing from the model and drawing and painting from nature were practised painstakingly, just as the pianist played his scales and the vocalist sang his *solfeggio*. Structure and virtuosity of technique were made ready for whatever came the artist's way as his experience and his reputation grew.

Marcia Brown, Caldecott Medal winner for several of her picture books, says "People speak of some artists who use different techniques as if they had fifty up their sleeves ready to appear, full-blown, when needed. But the life of an artist is one of constant preparation. He almost never feels that he has realized his aim. When a book is finished, he is usually just beginning to feel how it might have been. Stacks of trial drawings and rejects

attest to many efforts to find the right way to say what one has to say. One develops the technique necessary to express one's feeling about the particular book in hand. Sometimes this takes several months of drawing into a subject until one is ready to begin the actual illustrations. People often ask how much time it takes to make a book. Five days, five months, three years — as long as is necessary to get down one's ideas and feelings about the book."[3]

It is interesting to note how many accomplished and successful artists speak of the challenge of the *next* book — as the chance to perfect what they feel the last one may have lacked.

In the days of pre-offset book production, when most artwork was prepared for line cuts or half-tone color plates printed on shiny paper, no one expected to illustrate a book with artwork achieved by cutting and pasting bits of paper, or by zapping in the background with an airbrush. Note: I am not saying collage, or the special effects achieved with an airbrush (or with "light areas . . . created with water and bleach applied with a brush" to water colors already applied to paper "with cotton" — Leo and Diane Dillon's artwork for *The Hundred Penny Box* by Sharon Bell Mathis is described as being prepared thus) are necessarily wrong, although they seem to have arrived in the children's book field through the influence of voluptuous artwork done for advertising. What I am saying is there are many choices of media: When it comes to specific books, I wish they were always well-considered choices.

For example, I think of the line or ink-line-and-water color work of Joseph Low, and I sense behind it a continuity — from Caldecott to Rackham to Shepard to Ardizzone, and on to Low, Blegvad, and Sendak. Sendak in particular has acknowledged the inspiration of Caldecott's work — and not just the quality of his line and drawing. For Sendak, Caldecott's "greatness lies in the truthfulness of his personal vision . . ." and he goes on to point out that "Truthfulness to life — both fantasy life and factual life — is the basis of all great art."[4] Or I look at the beautifully modeled figures done by Symeon Shimin and Anthony Ravielli and

1 Henry C. Pitz, *The Brandywine Tradition*, Boston, Houghton Mifflin Company, 1969, pp. 117-118.

2 Thomas Handforth, "Personal Progress Toward the Orient," *The Horn Book Magazine*, July-August 1939, p. 245.

3 Marcia Brown, "My Goals as an Illustrator," *The Horn Book Magazine*, June 1967, p. 311.

4 Maurice Sendak, "Caldecott Award Acceptance," *The Horn Book Magazine*, August 1964, pp. 346, 347.

behind it sense the solid drawing of Pyle and N. C. Wyeth. I wish that young illustrators today had a wider background of apprenticeship and experience from which to make their choices; that collage was only chosen for an illustration because it was exactly right for that special story, not just because the artist had always wanted to do a book in collage or lacked sensitive drawing ability; that an airbrush was used because no other means could achieve a specific effect — not because it was a kick to use one and a much speedier method of blue-skying than Maxfield Parrish's slow perfectionist painting.

It is discouraging to find that this antithesis between fine art and illustration still exists today. In one of the most prestigious art schools on the East Coast the Illustration Department recently offered not one course, nor even part of a course, on making separations for color work. A course in film animation techniques was available in that department and was very popular. But it was not considered necessary for a student to have the experience of working up an illustration for mechanical reproduction, through the use of light-boxes, overlays, register marks, and discovering at firsthand the very subtle and often discouraging problems of working out in black and grays the tones which would eventually be printed in blues, yellows, and reds, and in shades thereof. I asked a former dean of this school why there was such a blind lack of technical training in such a famous school — one where the tuition was so high that a student needed to graduate with all the skills his chosen field could require. His reply was that the school expected that such details as separation techniques could be learned elsewhere; the philosophy being that the student spent his valuable time at the school being an artist — not a laborer (and the tedium of making separations can be laborious) or technician (even though making separations involves highly skilled techniques and sensitivities). But where else is the student to learn? On the job? In these day of fierce competition for art assignments? The student still had to spend more money going to a technical school or taking a night course to pick up those vital details of making separations.

Needless to say, making separations of color work is what separates the professionals from the amateurs — and those few who have arrived at the top and are allowed to do their originals in full color from those still making their way up. Three articles on the subject are included in this volume in Section III: "Color Separation" by Adrienne Adams; "Color Separation: The Use of Photostats" by Juliet Kepes; and "Combining Dinobase and Wash on Paper" by Dahlov Ipcar.

Which brings us to the opposite side of the problem — the technical schools that provide artists with facility in a variety of media but very little background in the history and philosophy of art, in liberal arts (after all, the artist has to have something to express and a point of view about it), or in aesthetics. Philosophy and aesthetics are as much a part of the illustration of children's books as the story, the typography, and the various kinds of illustration — from realistic to expressionistic.

"For the picture book illustrator there is no point in trying to be purely representational," write Donnarae MacCann and Olga Richard. "The meaning in his picture comes from the way he arranges colors, lines, shapes, and textures into a special synthesis, one that will please the senses and provide an aesthetic experience for the reader. Object recognition is a criterion based on the commonplace. It is concerned with simple imitation. The arts are the very antithesis of commonplace standards of imitation, recognition, and the sense of familiarity derived from such considerations. . . ."[5] "Looking at picture-book illustrations, a six-year-old noticed that the girl carrying the bucket in Frasconi's illustration in *The House That Jack Built* gave the feeling of being 'in a big hurry.' 'There's a rushing feeling from the way the body is placed.' 'It leans on the edge of the paper.' Marcia Brown's familiar portrait of Cinderella was seen as lonely, soft, gentle. 'The colors are put on fuzzy.' 'The lines stop sometimes and that makes it soft, too.' Evidence pointing to the aesthetic sensitivity of children can be gathered on all sides."[6]

Perhaps the biggest lack of all, however, for the artist who has only a technical school background is that he may have little knowledge of the field of children's literature, which, aside from book jackets, paperback and record album covers, cartoons, and artwork for advertising and packaging, is the main area of work open to an illustrator today.

5 Donnarae MacCann and Olga Richard, *The Child's First Books, A Critical Study of Pictures and Texts*, New York, The H. W. Wilson Company, 1973, p. 24.

6 MacCann and Richard, *The Child's First Books*, pp. 6-7.

Art directors in publishing companies look for an artist sensitive to the style of a particular story. "Each piece of writing has a beat," Walter Lorraine, Director of Juvenile Books at Houghton Mifflin, writes in expressing his view of illustrators, "a rhythm that is uniquely of that writing's particular world. The most effective illustrators can sense that beat and pick it up and then can play it back, jazz fashion, with exciting variations of expression brought from their own experiences that will enhance and extend the message.

"To best make this play, illustrators themselves must have considerable experience with life and be sensitive to it. But most essential, they must be able to read. Interpretation is the thing, a creative joining with the world of text. Far too many aspiring illustrators do not choose to read and therefore never understand the basic concept of illustration.

"I mean this in a symbolic sense. Of course they read the text and possibly do get the facts straight but they come to that text more to impose their will upon it rather than to interact openly with it — a jazz player with a totally foreign beat to the music at hand."[7]

This sensitivity to the beat, the rhythm of words and sentence structure, the style of the story, used to be developed subconsciously during long hours of childhood reading, which later provided invaluable insight for the older generation of artists still illustrating today. In writing about their lives and work, most of them have emphasized this personal development.

Younger artists brought up in an era of growing visual excitement (from Disney's *Fantasia* to such programs as PBS's International Animation Festival; from the original *King Kong* to Fellini's *Satyricon;* from Rojankovsky's *Daniel Boone* to Ungerer's *Allumette*) and even visual violence (fluorescent day-glo colors, strobe light and the "one-hundred-frames-in-twenty-seconds" effects), especially those who spent their childhood watching television rather than reading, have never developed ears for this beat. Moreover, their eyes are calibrated to rapid movement of image and design, extreme color contrasts, and such short segments in which to grab attention that all the nuances of a subject must be compressed into immediately recognizable visual symbols. This visual experience is very often out-of-synch with its intended verbal accompaniment, and the young artist who knows little of literary tradition or art history becomes impatient with the "limitations" he feels imposed upon him by the material he might be asked to illustrate.

On the other hand, the new approaches to visual impact are important in the growth of audio-visual materials, films, and film-strips. How philosophy, aesthetics, knowledge of children's literature (myths and legends) and film-making can blend is a vital concept in the films and books of Gerald McDermott. His article, "On the Rainbow Trail," is included in Section IV, which considers both elements of communication — the message and the media. For the media aspects, which represent far more than graphic symbols, there are two articles on film-making, the one just referred to by McDermott, and "How the Sun and the Moon Got Into a Film" by Blair Lent.

As to the message, Dr. Bruno Bettelheim has said that picture books for three-to-five-year-olds should have a "clear, definite message." Also included in this section is "Within the Margins of a Picture Book" by Uri Shulevitz, in which he says, "A picture book is not a silly little plaything. It is much more. Sometimes it can be everything to a child. Its message, written in coded language, reaches the child in his prison, is understood by him while often hidden from the adult or the parent...." Although Shulevitz states "written in coded language" he interprets the illustrations as a vital element of that "coded language" — the young child being able to understand what he sees where he cannot always understand what he reads or hears.

Some of the discussions in this book are not new; but they are on-going and they are important. They convey ideas and concepts and background which could be helpful to the new generation of artists, not only to those whose art training is purely technical, but also to those whose main experience is heavily weighted toward the visual alone.

While we are considering the need to integrate visual and verbal attitudes when we discuss the problems of illustration, there is no doubt that the artist sees differently. His world is that of the 3-D of light-defining forms, even if he translates it into the 2-D of a painting, a print, or an illustration. An

7 Walter Lorraine, "On Illustrators — My View," *The Calendar*, Vol. XXXIV, No. 1, March-August 1975, The Children's Book Council, Inc., unpaged.

author, even though he may have the added gift of 3-D vision but not the ability to draw or paint, has to work in the linear medium — stringing words connecting sentences into paragraphs. That distinction between the mental conception and subsequent creation of artist and author is obvious. The disciplines and backgrounds of experience are different and one does not expect to find an art school also directing its attention to writers. The art school, technical or fine-arts oriented, should, however, stress the artist's need to be aware of far more than his personal vision.

Two purposes of this book have so far been set forth. First, that it will provide background — the ideas, lives, and philosophies of artists experienced in the children's book field — to those whose training is limited to a technical approach. Second, that it will give, in as far as it is possible to do so by words alone, some technical information about illustration — to those whose art training has slighted these aspects, or to those interested in learning about illustration on their own without formal training. That some illustrators have succeeded in teaching themselves is shown by the careers of such successful artists as Valenti Angelo and Dahlov Ipcar, whose comments appear in Sections II and III. It is also encouraging to see the ability with which artists add to their repertoires, when those who began their careers in sculpture, as did Louis Slobodkin, or furniture design, as did Edwin Tunis, turn to illustration. Many artists who start as easel and mural painters, or support themselves with advertising artwork, have also become illustrators. Artists fortunately do not seem to see the same barriers between disciplines as art schools do, for which we can indeed be thankful.

I hope there are other things this book will accomplish, too. One is to minimize the distinction made between fine art, high art, or "pure" art — however it is phrased — and the art of illustration. Nancy Hale, an experienced and gifted writer who is the daughter of painters, grew up absorbing both language and art. She is a good verbal interpreter of visual concerns. She writes in her biography of Mary Cassatt: "If a non-painter will assemble the meager group of objects that have impressed themselves on his vision in the last half-hour, strain out of them all meaning (he won't be able to, entirely), and imagine that these objects, taken together do say something, though not in

words, which, if he were a painter he would apprehend — he may catch a glimpse of the language of art, tantamount to hearing with one's own ears Chinese being spoken when one does not understand Chinese.

"One reason why 'serious artists' . . . generally refer with a certain contempt to illustrators is that art is not illustrating anything, at least in the outside world. It illustrates that it is. The greater part of those viewing a given exhibition of pictures, including some art connoisseurs, assume the pictures to be illustrating at the very least verbal ideas, and meanings entertained by the artists beforehand. It is true, there have been painters who painted verbally expressive ideas (say, Daumier) but in their work there were other elements also, that escape the earnest searcher for a story. With great painters throughout the ages it was generally a matter of indifference what their subjects 'meant.' What did matter was shapes, colors, the relation of objects to adjoining objects, the values of lighted objects as against those less lighted. How the object looked was its story and its only story." [8]

Given the need for illustrators to be the best of artists and the need for illustrated books and picture books to have art of the highest quality, it is long past the time when fine artists should put down their fellow fine artists who also illustrate. Henry Pitz wrote about N. C. Wyeth: "He resented the implied barrier between illustration and painting. . . . Both the illustrator and painter, he believed, were artists engaged in pictorial communication. The illustrator, he knew, could reach a large audience, but he was hampered by size requirements and reproductive restrictions and limited in his choice of subject material. Both, he believed, should be measured by the degree of their talents, not by artificial compartments contrived by critics.

"Down the long perspective of the arts he could see that the illustrative, the narrative element had emerged strongly in the work of master after master, from Giotto to Rubens, Grünewald to Blake, Dürer to Daumier, Breugel to Delacroix, from the cave paintings of Ajanta to Japanese prints." [9]

8 Nancy Hale, *Mary Cassatt,* Garden City, New York, Doubleday & Company, Inc., 1975, p. 37.

9 Pitz, *The Brandywine Tradition,* p. 203.

A credo for artists and art schools might well be the words Walter Lorraine wrote in his Introduction to "The Artist at Work" series (see Section III) : "Art that serves the function of illustration, yet transcends the mundane to bring a new dimension of experience to the viewer, is not lightly conceived. It can only be born from the individual creative artist's private compulsion. It is not possible to specify as a condition for publication that an author write artistically, nor is it possible to specify that a piece of illustration must be art. It *is* or *is not*, depending on the sensibilities of the artist involved and his response to the text." [10]

Another purpose of this book is to encourage those still struggling between art school and finding a foothold in a career of illustration not to give up. It is harder than ever now to get assignments or to have a picture book published. Publishing, both trade and educational, is still reflecting the discouraging pinch of inflation and continually rising costs, and fewer books are being put out now than there were even five years ago. Success so rarely happens overnight. Part of the present failure of young artists who have great potential to keep on trying is the result of the insistence of today's society on instant gratification or recognition (or, alas, needed instant financial recompense.) Perhaps this book will give a longer view by recognizing how time and maturity will help.

Henry Pitz also wrote with great sympathy of these problems which beset young artists, when he described Pyle's early problems. "For the artist the whole process of bridging the gap from imitative recording to creative freedom requires a revolution both in thought and execution. The process has often been described as 'unlearning what one has learned.'

"Pyle made the transition from imitative to original art gradually and with difficulty. He suffered through a period of trial and error, making hopeful experiments and experiencing disheartening failures; there were many times when the whole thing seemed of little worth. This period affected him deeply. When he finally achieved the artistic solutions that accorded with his inmost nature, he had arrived at bedrock convictions that governed his creative lifetime as a picture maker and permeated every moment of his subsequent teaching. He began to have trust in his imagination and let his artist's appraising eye be its servant." [11]

There are several surveys useful to those wishing to acquaint themselves with the children's picture book field. One is a short work by a British critic, Brian Alderson, *Looking at Picture Books 1973*, which is a catalog with an introduction and commentary about an exhibition of picture books prepared by Brian Alderson for the National Book League in London; the catalog is distributed in the United States by the Children's Book Council,[12] and major libraries should have it in their reference collection. The second is an insightful comprehensive study by an American critic, Barbara Bader, *American Picturebooks from Noah's Ark to the Beast Within* (Macmillan, 1976), wherein the trends, influences, developments and styles of all the major American illustrators since the 1920s are put in perspective. There is also a perceptive book by Donnarae MacCann and Olga Richard, *The Child's First Books, A Critical Study of Pictures and Texts* (Wilson, 1973). Particularly valuable, too, are original sketches, dummies, and finished artwork donated by artists to collections such as The Kerlan Collection at the University of Minnesota and the Lena Y. de Grummond Collection at the University of Southern Mississippi. Quite a few other universities and some major libraries also have original artwork which may be seen and studied on request.

All of the material in the body of this book comes from *The Horn Book Magazine* or books published by The Horn Book, Incorporated. It has been a great temptation to add pertinent material from other sources. But space does not permit, and even the material used here has been severely pruned in some cases. Omitted as well are the often fascinating acceptance speeches by winners of the Caldecott Medal, which may be found printed annually, since 1938, in the August issues of *The Horn Book Magazine*, as well as in *Caldecott Medal Books: 1938-1957*, edited by Bertha Mahony Miller and Elinor Whitney Field; and *Newbery and Caldecott Medal Books 1956-1965* and *Newbery and Caldecott Medal Books: 1966-1975*,

---

10 Walter Lorraine, "Introduction," "The Artist at Work," *The Horn Book Magazine*, December 1963, p. 576-577.

11 Pitz, *The Brandywine Tradition*, pp. 44-45.

12 Children's Book Council, Inc., 67 Irving Place, New York, N.Y. 10003.

both edited by Lee Kingman, all published by The Horn Book, Inc.

Please note, however, that these articles and excerpts for illustrators do not attempt to give a complete guide to all the techniques available to artists. New methods are frequently developed. Some stay, some don't (for example, the fluorescent paint of the 1940s which was supposed to make camera-separation of color easier for the printer, but was not at all good for the artist using it, especially if he forgot and put his paint brush in his mouth). Rather, these articles give an artist's experience and use of some of the techniques. Nor is this a definitive volume on all the problems inherent in illustrating a book: for example, one will have to look elsewhere for notes on book jackets and details about typography.

The reader will also find material presenting conflicting points of view presented by different artists. There is no attempt to make a simplistic approach to illustration.

Some may wonder why some of the material quoted is taken from articles originally written as long ago as 1930. The answer is obvious: it is still relevant and often a more original expression than that of more recent writers on the same theme. Also, as Walter Lorraine writes: "A good illustrator's work, though it may have the flavor of its time, will always be fresh in its content and story-telling quality."[13] This applies to words on the subject as well as pictures. New generations of artists can now discover a heritage from other artists, no less cogent for having stood the test of time.

The editor hopes this book will also be useful to authors who need insight into the problems their writing creates for illustrators, and to librarians and students in the children's literature field interested in the creative processes that result in fine illustrative art.

---

[13] Lorraine, ''On Illustrators — My View,'' *The Calendar.*

I

Notes on the History and
Philosophy of Illustration,
Its Standards, and
Its Place in the Arts

The Education of an Artist

by Fritz Eichenberg

To speak of the education of an illustrator seems to me to give too much honor to an undesirable by-product of our age — specialization. To put first things first: the illustrator is an artist whose education knows no beginning and no end.

He belongs to an ancient and honorable lineage; his ancestry goes back into the dim past. The sum total of the experiences, skills, and insights of his predecessors is in his blood when he is born. This total is a compound of the imagery of the cave artist, of the tribal artisan in an African village, of the pictorial recorder of Pharaoh's exploits, of the medieval illuminator of the Gospel — and down through the ages to our own abstract interpretations of nuclear nightmares.

The artist not only *sees* the world around him, he *feels* its tremors by dint of his supersensitivity, and records them long before society takes official cognizance of them. The real artist, the innovator, is far ahead of his time. This makes him the "Odd One" — a nonconformer, and as such in many ways a social outcast.

The artist's education, I said, never ends. He gathers impressions incessantly; he perfects his

Fritz Eichenberg is an artist who has been working in the field of book illustration in the United States for over thirty-five years. As Professor of Art, he has taught at Pratt Institute in Brooklyn where he also served as Chairman of the Department of Graphic Art and Illustration. Well-known for his illustration of a series of classics for the Limited Editions Club, he has also illustrated a number of books for children. The following remarks were first given at a conference on "A Study of Eye Appeal in Children's Books," held at Pratt Institute, Brooklyn, in 1959.

tools to transform them into visual images; he works on his own spiritual and individual perfection unceasingly, always reaching beyond his present capacities, and so is rarely satisfied with his own performances.

What emerges finally from the crucible may, at its best, be a daring innovation, an artist's most personal and revelatory expression, and, at its most trivial, a style easily recognized, catalogued, evaluated, and imitated.

As art is formed by the artist's mind, heart, and hand, it in turn molds and influences the modes and manners of the society in which he lives. It can give form to that rare and evasive phenomenon, the taste of a nation; it can also deform it. It is a fascinating interplay of cause and effect, motivated by psychohistoric forces, as Walter Abell defined it in his penetrating *The Collective Dream in Art* (Harvard University Press, 1957).

The artist tries to express his generation's dreams, bedded deep down in our collective subconscious. If we are outraged by contemporary art in its most nightmarish aspects, we should be equally outraged by the time in which we live, by the contaminated air we breathe, by the suicidal political games we play.

If senselessness, futility, ugliness, distortion have invaded contemporary art, they have also permeated our daily lives, and the artist seems to be the only one sensitive enough to express them, to hold them up in a reflection for all to see.

My plea, then, is for a public with an open mind, for the open mind is essential to arrive at the truth, or at least a fraction of it. We can profit only by expanding our knowledge through constant search, and the artist may well be the "little child who will lead us."

Since we have to narrow our discussion to illustration, that much abused stepchild of the arts, we must realize that it is just one page taken out of the colorful, fascinating, many chaptered volume we call art.

To escape the strait jacket of specialization the artist has to explore the vast potentialities of *all* the media of expression; he has to search the past, venture into the future, and transform the present world of sight, form, and texture into a world of his own creation.

1. Illustration by Fritz Eichenberg for *Heroes of the Kalevala* by Babette Deutsch, Messner, 1940.

He may consider the vocation of a painter, a sculptor, a printmaker; or of an actor, a playwright or a poet; or a combination of all these experiences. He may want to become a student of history, of science, of philosophy — of all the humanities which are our cultural heritage — and engage himself in unending studies which are finally woven into the fabric that makes an artist's work great and timeless.

The artist as an illustrator has to be a literate person, with a love and respect for the written word, with the gift to interpret it pictorially, with the discipline to subordinate himself to it, and with the skill to adapt his technique to the requirements of the book.

To be more specific: as an illustrator of children's books he must have a deep love for and understanding of the child; he must be neither condescending nor too involved intellectually.

Sensitivity, humor, excitement, imagination, warmth of heart are prerequisites, as the *lack* of them would disqualify any artist for working with or for children.

More and more of our contemporary artists are discovering in the children's book a challenge and an adventure. To them it represents the chance to design a book as an entity, splash color across its pages, be able to control, to a degree, the whole production of a book, and to be assured of a certain permanency, of a purity of purpose, of a "Thing of Value."

Where else can we counteract the corroding fear that seems to paralyze our generation but in the young mind which still imagines the world as a pristine creation, full of promise, excitement, and beauty? Where else can we, the adults, recapture our own childhood, meet with our children in their own world, without loss of dignity, without feeling foolish or rejected?

... This may sound all too glamorous but there is a debit side to it, as can be expected. One disadvantage is, oddly enough, the profit system which makes publishing possible. It tends to exploit the successful artist, extract from him book after book, modeled after the image of his first success.

How much success can the artist stand, how much the market? There is a definite saturation point for both, unless the artist is allowed a certain amount of experimentation which will keep him mindful of his own development and keep the public interested in new variations of a theme.

The second drawback is the flood of imitators, often promoted and fostered by competing publishers, which reduces a fresh style to a worn-out formula.

The third is the avalanche of trashy books, those perverters of good taste, poorly produced, illustrated and designed — a horror to the eye, scaring off good artists who otherwise might want to try their hand in the children's book field.

It seems to me a thing of great importance to make illustration not so much a profession as an adventure to be constantly renewed and replenished by a new growth. It is as important to encourage artists of proven stature to try their hand as illustrators as it is to foster young talent graduating from the best art schools in the country.

Every book should be a work of art, a thing of beauty, aimed at permanency.

But the children's book especially should be considered for its impact on the young mind — a conveyor of good taste and of all the finest things which are the ingredients of our culture, and an antidote to the creeping horrors of our time.

From *The Horn Book Magazine*, February 1960.

2. Illustration by Madeleine Gekiere for *Grimm's Tales* illustrated by Helen Sewell and Madeleine Gekiere, Oxford, 1954.

Contemporary Book Illustration

by Lynd Ward

In the early days of bookmaking, men approached the problems of type and picture with minds free of all considerations save that of making a book. Then gradually the creation of the illustrations was separated from the rest, became involved, complex, a goal in itself. Reproduction entered in, first in the form of human craftsmanship and then, by human ingenuity, in the form of cold machines. Undreamed-of possibilities suddenly leaped upon the scene and after some years . . . we found that what we were offering as illustration for books was far from being book illustration. So, heartened by a revolt already won against somewhat similar conditions in Europe, we slowly, carefully, craftily, unobtrusively revolted.

Many, of course, will deny that there has been any revolt. . . . But the fact remains that the prevailing and most prominent characteristics of book art today are so far a cry from the situation of twenty

In 1930, when he wrote the following article, Lynd Ward was already known as the creator of Gods' Man, *a book told entirely by its illustrations, there being no text. He was also one of the first to express a philosophy of illustration for those working in the field of children's books. Today Lynd Ward is known as a winner of the Caldecott Medal (1953) for* The Biggest Bear *and as the illustrator of more than seventy books for children. His remarks on "Contemporary Book Illustration," written not quite half a century ago, were made just as the opportunities for artists to place their work were changing from the heavily illustrated periodicals of the previous half century to a greater use of illustration in books — particularly children's books. Lynd Ward not only felt the vitality of this change, he helped to create it, and even though "contemporary" in his title refers to the 1930s, much of what he had to say about the purpose of illustration is still pertinent today.*

years ago as to be practically in revolutionary relation to them. And the foremost book artists of today have won their position and established the essential right of their beliefs by a not altogether easy struggle.

There is by no means a consistent character throughout the field. But the leaders, the people whose work is regarded as outstanding and representative of the best that we have, do, fortunately, determine the tangible character of the field. In them undeniably, we have a new world.

Your outstanding contemporary book illustrator is a different man from his immediate predecessors. He is, to begin with, very seriously concerned with his work as a serious artist. He is no dabbler, no superficial trafficker in sentimentalities. The day of the pretty drawing, the careful, uninspired and pretty penwork, the large and literal oil painting, is over. . . .

The book artist of today is concerned with technique in a far more significant way than were those to whom technique meant, for example, developing the ability to handle a pen so meticulously as to overshadow in complexity the master Aubrey Beardsley. Your contemporary carries his study of book technique to its source, and instead of asking "How far can I go and still get the stuff between book covers by means of complex reproduction?" he demands of himself, "What modern processes have been developed that are logically suited to the creation of work that is pure book?"

The answering of this question has carried him directly into the craftsmanship of bookmaking, the best possible place for an illustrator to be. He has discovered that type and picture meet at definite points in their development, that one is designed essentially in the same way as the other is designed; the problem of unity is made clearer. Your contemporary is, therefore, in exactly the same relation to his work as were the early bookmakers, whose products have for centuries been held up as most nearly approaching the perfect form. Stimulated by that realization, his illustration has attained a simplicity and an undiluted book quality that has never been achieved in any other way.

When, in his search into the technique of illustration, your contemporary finds himself back at the starting point of the book as a distinct phenom-

3, 4. Illustrations by Lynd Ward for
Gods' Man A Novel in Woodcuts by
Lynd Ward, Jonathan Cape and
Harrison Smith, 1929.

enon, he cannot help realizing the necessity of treating the book as a single unit from binding design to tailpiece. . . . His illustrations, then, are inevitably of a different quality, a part of the flesh of the book in their technical creation, a part of the spirit of the book in the way they have come into being.

The result of this fundamental approach has been a body of work that is pure book illustration, an achievement infinitely rarer than one would suppose. . . .

If at some time in the misty future an interested gentleman looks back upon our present age, he must surely note the quality of prizing the original spirit as the most valuable we have developed. It is,

I believe, intrinsically bound up with a right regard for the medium. The two go along together and sustain each other. . . .

Most impressive, perhaps, of the many ways in which the new vitality evidences itself is the growing importance of the artist as a functional being rather than a mere complementary decorator. For some years a philosophy of book illustration has contended that the business of the artist is limited to the creation of a pleasing (usually pretty) accompaniment of the essential fiber of the story. No artist with a serious understanding of what he is doing can ever accept that restriction of his book function . . . in many cases the artist has succeeded in making his contribution to the book, not

6

only quite as important as the original text, but often the vital life fluid of the story. And heartened perhaps by his ability to do that, or possibly out of sheer exuberance, he has developed the picture book as a recognized and by now very necessary part of literature. . . .

What [the picture book] is, essentially, is a capitalization of the literary qualities that are inherent in every unit of visual art. The artist has made the not-altogether-wild conjecture that if a writer lists in his text certain qualities that are to be included in the development of a certain character, a picture of that character in which those qualities are foremost would carry the message equally well, if not better, and it would then be a simple step to dispense with the list of qualities in the text. By thus paring down and building up, processes quite congenial to the making of an illustration, the artist is able to tell a story in which the usual relation of much text to little picture is exactly reversed and the greatest part of the story is told by the pictures themselves. There are both anthropological and psychological bolsterings for this development and the fact that increasing numbers of artists are finding in it a place for intelligent activity promises much for the future.

Intelligent activity is the prerequisite of art.

Excerpts from the article which appeared in *The Horn Book Magazine*, February 1930.

Illustration Today in Children's Books

by Warren Chappell

Creation is adventure. Regardless of how often the trials are made, it is not humanly possibly to materialize imagination. Artists then can never hope to sense the full satisfaction that can come to an able craftsman. To be sure, there is a good deal of craft in illustration; one must work for a printed result, and the job is done only when the presses stop rolling. But it is the elusive creative admixture which keeps the greatest technique from being empty. One of the gravest dangers facing any illustrator is the pigeonhole, for though it may aid his ability to produce in quantity, it stifles both the creative capacity and the very natural enthusiasm of adventure.

It should be obvious that there is no such thing as an expert, that experience carries with it such a broadening of vision that it vitiates any tendency toward becoming almighty. Whether the pigeonhole or the individual artist is responsible for today's plethora of tired illustrations, it is difficult to say. One thing, however, is certain — the superior attitude, the attitude of talking down to the audience, can never produce good work.

An illustration is a pictorial statement. It should never be a technical manipulation, and only in the rarest of descriptive instances should it be a costume exercise. Hollywood has shown us that it is possible to serve up costumes which, though correct in every detail, fail completely to be clothes and to be worn as such.

Every illustrator must of necessity have a method, and he should be aware of the vast background of pictorial art with all its devices of composition and means for describing shapes. This knowledge, however, cannot lessen the anxiety with which he must approach each piece of work, large or small. How often, as praise, one hears a comment on an illustrator's technique, and yet the very fact that it has called attention to itself suggests a mannerism. The artist's method should only be apparent to another artist.

Warren Chappell, who has designed type faces and written books about calligraphy, printing, type and illustration, is strongly concerned with the production of the book as a complete unit. His special talents for illustration and book design are well displayed in the musical series printed by Knopf, including Coppelia *(1965),* The Magic Flute *(1962), and* The Ring *(1964).*

5, 6. Illustrations by Warren Chappell for *The Nutcracker* adapted and illustrated by Warren Chappell, Knopf, 1958, 9⅝ x 7¼.

twelve. At the final stroke noises came from the parlor. There was a clinking of swords, a scurry of feet—then silence. Presently she heard a soft knock at her door, and a soft little voice asked her to open it. She swiftly opened the door, and there stood Nutcracker, sword in hand.

He beckoned Marie to follow him. Together, they went to a closet in the hall. From a sleeve of one of Judge Silberhaus's coats Nutcracker pulled down a little stairway. They had no sooner set foot upon the stairs than they were transported onto a perfumed meadow, which glittered and gleamed as if it were strewn with precious stones.

It was the Plain of Sugar Candy. Nutcracker led Marie through a splendid door made of orange-flower conserve, pralines, and raisins. It opened on a gallery supported by columns of sugared orange and paved with pistachios and macaroons. They journeyed on and came to the Christmas Forest, in which some of the trees were covered with snow and lit with thousands of candles. Others were hung with fruits of many colors.

Marie wanted to stop and enjoy the wonder of this place. Nutcracker clapped his hands, and shepherds and shepherdesses, hunters and huntresses came out of the forest. They were like tinted Dresden figurines that had come to life. A stool of nougat candy was brought for Marie, and then a

Dance of th Reed Pipes

... The part played by typography in the making of children's books can be overestimated, but it has a definite role. Just as the individual picture must be organized within itself, so is the relationship of these individual pictures in the whole scheme a part of the problem. And just as the individual illustration should not be design-ridden, so the whole is not improved by self-conscious typographic treatment. The finished book must not elicit the comment that it is a good-looking package — that's merchandising language, not critical.

Illustrators should be interested in the past, and should learn from it. The idea of originality is an invention of progressive education. Shakespeare and Molière drew on their forerunners, Rubens spent much of his time in Spain copying paintings in the Prado, and Rembrandt made dozens of copies of Persian miniatures. In each case the result was something new. It cannot be said too often that art thrives on continuity, and that the work of any individual becomes a part of the general heritage....

An artist should be encouraged to illustrate around most of the main passages of a manuscript, rather than laboriously to reconstruct those scenes which often are already adjective-laden and overdescribed. After all, the artist is a collaborator, and his task is a complementary one.

Illustrations fall roughly into three groups: narrative, descriptive, and decorative. In the first cate-gory is to be found the greatest work, the illustrations with true literary content. Here the illustrator is making a contribution from his own experience and creates a story held in suspense among the various characters and objects of his composition. Descriptive illustrations range from a diagram of a monkey wrench to a battle scene by Meissonier. The decorative classification runs from Burne-Jones to wallpaper. There are not more than a half-dozen designers today who can do really fine decorations, so it is safe to conclude that book illustration in this last category has everything against it at the outset.

... When one considers the comics, the movie cartoons, and the textbooks, it is safe to say that the average child's pictorial experience is all but bankrupt, and that a good ninety-five percent of the illustration he sees is little more than competent art student work. This is not to underestimate the art student's work; it is simply to say that time and maturity add something completely beyond the realm of technique, and that through living himself, an artist is able to bring life and reality to his characters and his statements about them. Realism is a very different thing. It is reality which can be created by experienced minds and hands.

Excerpts from the article which first appeared in *The Horn Book Magazine*, November-December 1941.

ther's

ry

THE next evening Godfather Drosselmayer came to see Marie. He sat beside her bed, and told her a story, to explain how Nutcracker and the Mouse King had become enemies.

IN a small country, not far from Nuremberg, a beautiful baby girl was born to the King and Queen. Her hair was long and golden, and her teeth pearly white. The King and Queen named her Pirlipate.

The Queen said she must be guarded all of the time, so she was watched over by six strong nursemaids who sat around the cradle, each with a cat in her lap. These unusual measures were taken because of Dame Souriconne, the Mouse Queen. Many months before the Princess was born the Mouse Queen had vowed to cast a spell on the first-born of the royal couple.

This was all because the King was very fond of sausages. When the Court Astrologer told him the time was right for sausage-making, he asked the Queen to prepare them in the way she had always done. While the Queen was in the kitchen preparing a large quantity of pork for the King's favorite dish, Dame Souriconne appeared from her home beneath the hearth. She begged for some of the meat. Out of kindness, the Queen gave her a juicy morsel. But the delicious odor attracted the Mouse Queen's seven sons and

Through an Illustrator's Eyes

by Hilda van Stockum

... It is quite possible to have the artist hurt, and the author flattered, in the same person with a violent quarrel going on inside, the author crowing: "What do you expect? You're only a kind of appendix, entirely unnecessary, while *I* do the creative work." And the artist retorting bitterly: "You think you're hot, don't you? It's easy to write; anybody can WRITE. But just think of the years of

7. Illustration by George Cruikshank for *Sketches by "Boz"* by Charles Dickens, Chapman, 1839.

study it takes to draw a dog that doesn't look like a monkey upside down! Besides if I hadn't pointed up those feeble passages of yours and given some semblance of reality to your shadowy heroine, nobody would want to read your beastly little book!" These disputes are most uncomfortable, but they give one an idea of the problems involved. As usual, the truth lies somewhere in the middle.

The author *does* need the illustrator. It is a terrible bore to have to write long descriptions. . . . It is much easier to jot down in the margin "Picture of such and such," and have done with it. . . .

. . . The engravings in Dickens' Household Edition are a perfect example of the art of illustrating. They tell the story you're reading, not some other story the artist prefers. One even suspects the illustrator read the book, perhaps more than once. The people in the pictures are the same as in the book, with some details added which the author forgot to mention, and the pictures are placed where and when you expect them, at satisfying climaxes and dramatic moments, taking care of situations the author had to leave in a hurry. . . . He can't develop an intricate plot and bring it to an exciting explosion with everything happening at once unless he leaves some things to look after themselves. It is at those moments, when the author has to drop everything to rush after his story, that the illustrator must rise to the occasion and put the baby to bed, warm the soup, sweep the floor and show that the rest of the world is going on as usual.

In the same way the illustrator needs the author. He needs a good story with plenty of action and character and plenty of open space where he can put in his solo work. . . . But such teamwork is only achieved at a cost. If your artist insists on being a rugged individualist and picking out of the story only the plums to his liking, with complete disregard of the author's intentions, putting in a picture of a basket because he likes drawing baskets and not because it is of any significance, or avoiding the

Hilda van Stockum is known as both artist and author, and so is particularly qualified to discuss the problems which arise in illustrating books. She came to illustration, however, after solid academic training at an art school in Dublin and at the Academy of Art in Amsterdam, where she studied lithography and portrait painting.

great climax because it takes place in a church and he thinks it would be a bore to draw all those arches, then he may be an excellent draughtsman or easel painter, but he'll never make an illustrator.

To illustrate a book you have to absorb its message and its spirit. . . .

. . . When a book presents a perfect marriage of text and pictures, let no man put it asunder! But it must be a true marriage and not one of those flippant combinations which are sometimes sold as illustrated books. . . . The combination of a first-rate author and a first-rate artist working in complete harmony is one of the most beautiful things in the world, and very often it surpasses anything an author-artist can do by himself. As my old teacher used to say, "The more diverse the elements you bring together, the greater the beauty in the end."

. . . Having given the work of separate artist and author some of the attention it deserves, I should like to add a plea for the author-artist book too. If it seldom rises to the pitch which two people can achieve together, neither does it sink to as low a level of disharmony. In the author-artist book there is an intimate and contented companionship between text and illustrations which is pleasing to children, who usually fret at the slightest discrepancy between a story and its pictures.

. . . It [is] hard to value pictures properly. Not only does one have to consider the competence of an artist at his craft, but also what he is trying to express. Add to that his unconscious style, his "handwriting," and you have a compound picture of which there are infinite variations. The most important thing in my eyes, however, is that a drawing should have some kind of life, whether it is that the artist is particularly charmed with the furry grace of an animal, or whether he delights in humorous sketches, or prefers to emulate the expansive sweep of the cosmos. It must have a reason for being other than that the artist was asked to make it. It must reveal something of the author's personality or emotions, if it be only a passionate delight in curves. . . . Perfection of treatment is entirely subordinate in my opinion to this all-important quality. Let it be a scrawl, a scribble or a smudge, but at least let it *say* something. . . .

. . . A child does not forget. What he sees young he sees for his whole life. When he is older, he learns to look and forget; but at the age when he still pores over a picture book he is gathering treasures which he stores in odd pockets of his mind. . . .

Excerpts from the article which appeared in *The Horn Book Magazine*, May 1944.

8. Illustration by Hilda van Stockum for *Canadian Summer* written and illustrated by Hilda van Stockum, Viking, 1948.

An Illustrator's Viewpoint

by Barbara Cooney

Adornment of the written or printed word, illustration as we call it, is an ancient practice, an art not to be dismissed lightly. I use the word "art" because I believe illustration is, or should be, an art. Too much distinction is made today between "fine art" and "applied art," between "fine art" and "commercial art." Somewhere between these terms hovers the word "illustration." Yet all these terms are of comparatively recent vintage in the history of art. In ancient Greece all art was covered by one word: *tekhne.* The classical artist used his skill where the need arose. The artist today whose pictures lie within book covers should work with as much care, skill, and understanding as the artist whose pictures hang on the wall in gold frames.

Fifteen centuries before Christ the text of the Egyptian papyrus rolls known as *The Book of the Dead*

9. Illustration by Barbara Cooney for *Little Women* by Louisa M. Alcott, Crowell, 1955.

was illustrated with brilliantly painted pictures. Illustrated books were not uncommon in early Rome. In the Middle Ages throughout Europe monks laboriously and lovingly ornamented their vellum pages, and in Persia the manuscripts were a delight to the eye. Now why did men take these pains to adorn their words? What was the function of this adornment? It was certainly something more than that of the alluring wrapping around a toffee candy; it was more than a "come-on" to entice people to read; it was more than just factual instruction. Books were adorned because they were treasures. They were the storehouses of wisdom, wit, beauty, and knowledge; and, as such, they were treated with reverence and made beautiful. The binding, the ornamentation, the illustration, the very letters themselves, all were made to be as beautiful as possible.

Decoration, then, is the first function of illustration. A second function that it often performs is that of elucidating or interpreting the text. A distinction must be made between mere pictorial representation or instruction and interpretation. Furthermore, while decoration does nothing more than decorate, elucidation must decorate as well as elucidate. These two principles apply as much to today's machine-produced books as they did to the Egyptian papyri and the manuscripts of the medieval world.

Certainly, the illustrated book is not a necessity. Neither is opera. Neither is the ballet. But is it not satisfying to see with one's eyes, to feel with one's hands, a book that is illustrated and printed well? Man's senses overlap. An idea can be communicated by literature, by music, by drama, by art, and by combinations of these, one art enhancing the other. How well an illustrator transfers an author's ideas to his own medium is the measure of his success as an illustrator. . . . Also, as a symphony can be variously interpreted by different conductors so

Barbara Cooney was the 1958 winner of the Caldecott Medal, received eighteen years after she first began illustrating books for children, for Chanticleer and the Fox. *Although she had a liberal arts education at Smith College, she was always interested in painting and drawing and attended the Art Students League in New York. She has now illustrated over 70 books.*

can a text be illustrated, and illustrated well, by different artists. *The Arabian Nights* and *Don Quixote* have had various successful interpretations. It is difficult to choose between the pictures Rackham and Shepard made for *The Wind in the Willows,* or between those made by Thomas Nason and Aldren Watson for *Walden.* As a composer can be dismayed over a bad interpretation or the poor execution of his music, so can an author be dismayed when his book is badly or thoughtlessly or incorrectly illustrated. But this does not discredit illustration as such. A book *jacket* may be likened to a candy wrapping, but not the illustration proper. The two principles, decoration and elucidation, remain as the true functions of illustration.

. . . Besides being aware of the complexity of producing a book, it might help an author whose words are likely to be illustrated to know a little about the problems of illustration itself. Assuming that the author has had his manuscript accepted by a good publisher, one immediate problem is the choice of an illustrator. He should be a competent artist and craftsman; he should be in sympathy with the text; and, of course, he should be available. The first duty of a good illustrator is to know his manuscript cold. No illustrator worth his salt makes factual mistakes, substitutes blond hair for brown or shirts for jackets.

Another problem confronting an illustrator is the distribution of the pictures throughout the book. These must be more or less evenly placed, not bunched together in groups with great stretches of unillustrated pages in between. They should flow through the book in a rhythm that is interesting to the eye, neither anticipating the action nor coming too long after it. A half-page drawing here, a full-page one there, here a spot, there a spot, and so on. The illustrator tries to vary his pictures somewhat as a movie director tries to vary his shots, to avoid monotony.

Excerpts from the article which appeared in *The Horn Book Magazine,* February 1961.

10. Illustration by Garth Williams for *Little House on the Prairie* by Laura Ingalls Wilder, Harper, 1953, 5½ x 8.

INDIANS IN THE HOUSE

the Indians. And she felt safer. But she couldn't help moving her head just a little, so that one eye peeped out and she could see the wild men.

First she saw their leather moccasins. Then their stringy, bare, red-brown legs, all the way up. Around their waists each of the Indians wore a leather thong, and the furry skin of a small animal hung down in front. The fur was striped black and white, and now Laura knew what made that smell. The skins were fresh skunk skins.

A knife like Pa's hunting-knife, and a hatchet like Pa's hatchet, were stuck into each skunk skin.

The Indian's ribs made little ridges up their bare sides. Their arms were folded on their chests. At last Laura looked again at their

INDIANS IN THE HOUSE

faces, and she dodged quickly behind the slab.

Their faces were bold and fierce and terrible. Their black eyes glittered. High on their foreheads and above their ears where hair grows, these wild men had no hair. But on top of their

Distinction in Picture Books

by Marcia Brown

What is a distinguished picture book? . . . From the flood of picture books that pour off the presses each year it is increasingly difficult to select any that merit the designation "distinguished."

. . . The problem of choosing good illustration in the books we give our children has many ramifications in our contemporary life. A child can and must be trained in visual awareness if he is to become an aware adult. For the city child, there is the staccato excitement of geometry, subway lights, neon signs, sharp contrasts of light and shade, mass groupings of buildings and humanity. Human warmth becomes even more precious in such an atmosphere. For the country child there are the subtle curves of landscape, a close-up of seasonal changes, the design of plant forms, a chance to observe the relationship of the parts of nature to the whole. Each child can be taught to enlarge his horizons.

Taste, the ability to discriminate, to cast off the false, the unworthy, and to retain the genuine; the capacity to see what is before us, to be alert; the pleasure in what is harmonious and at the same time various; the poise that is born of inner rhythm

---

Many artists come to illustrating by roundabout routes. Although Marcia Brown had drawn and painted from childhood, she first attended New York State College for Teachers, Albany, and the Graduate School of Philosophy, Columbia University. She studied painting under Yasuo Kuniyoshi and Stuart Davis. She was a teacher; she worked in the New York Public Library. She is an articulate artist, both visually and verbally, well able to express her own philosophy and to explain the standards she feels important in the field of illustration.

and balance — all these are best formed in early childhood.

In our mechanized environment, mass media such as the comic book, the greeting card, magazine advertising, television, the motion picture and the animated cartoon influence the visual perception of a child. The child's avidity for information, his need for excitement and adventure, his imagination, are exploited in this mass production of taste, with all its accompanying paraphernalia of saccharinity, sadism, and frenzied destruction. Now, added to this we have the mass-produced . . . picture book that must cost as little as possible to produce and be easy to sell, since the motive for production is profit. . . .

Whether or not the author is artist, whether pictures and text form simultaneously in the author's mind or the writing of the text precedes the execution of the pictures, the problem of unity remains. For the pictures must be true to the spirit and feeling of the book as a whole, the spirit of the author's concept and the child's acceptance. Once the artist has grasped this concept . . . the plan of the book's appearance begins to take place in his mind. Perhaps he asks himself questions such as these:

What shape? How much space will I need for double spreads? Is the feeling of the book one of height, with tall buildings, trees that reach up, or is it horizontal, with long roads, the sea, a procession to stretch across a page? . . . What colors are appropriate to the story? Also, how many colors can the publisher afford to let me use? If I must use only two colors, what two will suggest the atmosphere of the story and provide one dark enough for a legible text? If the story has an exotic or historical background, how much of the style determined by the background shall I use in my pictures? What technique shall I use: fine line, reed pen, water color, flat color, wash and line, crayon, spatter, linoleum cut, pastel and line? What type face shall I keep in mind that will be harmonious with my drawings and also with the spirit of the book?

To anyone who has taken the trouble to show fine paintings or reproductions to little children it should be apparent that there need be no condescension to their ages in the types of drawing and painting we offer them. They embrace all kinds and all subjects freely. Their own drawings may be realistic, near abstract or conceptual. The child of six does not become lost in a tangle of associations and rules as he looks at a drawing. If its message is clear, whether simple or complex, he will comprehend it. Perhaps not all at once. But most worthwhile things bear more than one examination.

As for deciding which medium of illustration is best for children, the great variety of media and the many fine examples of each type prove the foolishness of dogmatism. The important question is what medium is best for this book, tells its message clearly — and is economically practicable. . . .

Nor can we make rules about color in children's books, except that it be harmonious and appropriate to the subject. We have become so saturated with color in our advertising, in our magazine illustration, and now in our motion pictures that we almost lose sight of the fact that children enjoy equally books with little or no color and books in full color. To refute the demand of those who want many colors, [consider] the richness of Wanda Gág's black and white drawings, [or] the sepia of [Robert McCloskey's] *Make Way for Ducklings.* . . . Color is not so important as the richness of the message told by the illustrations in these books so well liked by children.

At a time when production costs are [so high] the illustrator is obliged to become more skilled in the utilization of small amounts of color. He must know how to get everything out of his colors through overlays in his color separations. Some illustrators, like Nicolas Mordvinoff, Roger Duvoisin and Leo Politi, use two or three colors more effectively than others use five. The line drawings themselves must provide more color.

After the artist makes a dummy and has completed some of his final drawings he may help select a type face with the book designer or person in charge of manufacturing details. This type must be legible to children and harmonious with the pictures; it must fit into the proper space on the page and usually be available in linotype, since the cost of handset type is often prohibitive.

Before I worked on picture books I never realized the great number of manipulations that drawings and text go through before the completion of a book. I wish it were possible for everyone . . . to observe a large offset press in operation, to see how

11. Illustration by David Macaulay for *Cathedral The Story of Its Construction* written and illustrated by David Macaulay, Houghton Mifflin, 1973, 8⅞ x 11⅞.

negatives are made, how they are stripped up for making the final printing plates, and then to witness the actual printing of the large sheets that form the body of the book.

But from all the picture books produced, how are we to pick those which are exceptional? I believe that they must be regarded as are other forms of visual art. There is no recipe for judging illustration any more than there is a recipe for producing it. It is extremely difficult to be objective about a picture book because each of us brings something different to what he sees. What is beautiful to one of us might be merely dull to another. . . .

All that the artist has seen and felt deeply, his subconscious feelings and reactions to life, con-

15

tribute to his work and will often be discernible there, setting up similar reactions in us as we look at it. Some illustrations set up reactions that continue long after we have ceased to look at them. Others we grasp at a glance because of the very narrow range of the experience they offer. Some books for children can be returned to again and again, not only because the child enjoys the repetition, but because he will always find in them the reward of enjoyment.

In his *Last Lectures* Roger Fry suggests a method of examining works of art by confining attention to one or two qualities at a time and by comparing a number of different works to see to what extent they possess or lack these qualities. He chose sensibility and vitality. It might be profitable for us to study how these qualities can be reflected in the picture book.

The term sensibility includes two basic desires, the desire for order, harmony and the desire for variety, chance, the unexpected. The first is expressed in the overall design of a work, the coordination of the parts in the whole. The other is subject to the feeling and sensitivity of the artist in executing the design or plan.

... Without making set rules only to break them, let us subject the visual elements that compose a picture book to an examination for those qualities Fry suggests. We can learn something from asking ourselves questions such as these:

How appropriate are the illustrations to the spirit as well as the facts of the story? If the illustrations are merely decorations, is this treatment all the story demands? Is there extraneous gingerbread in the decoration that might better have been left out? Do treatments vary from page to page, or are many pages monotonously alike in design? Do the margins allow enough air for the pictures to move in? If the page is bled, is it best that way? Is the type legible and harmonious with the pictures and feeling of the story? Is there a pleasant visual play between pictures and type? Is the type attractively placed in relation to the pictures? Is the color appropriate, interesting, or watered-down, sugary? If it is bright and harsh, is it appropriate so? We can expect bright color from a fire engine or a circus. How has the illustrator seen the whole book in masses of color, in line, in rhythm? Why?

Is there a discernible build-up in the dramatic interest of the pictures as there is in the text? Is the characterization rich or meager, the people merely stereotypes, or do they have the qualities of individual human beings observable in life? Is there a build-up in characterization if the story requires it? Does the illustrator impose on us a reaction toward the characters that he wants us to feel? Does he nudge us to say, "This child, or this puppy, isn't he charming?" . . . If pushed too far we are apt to be aware of nothing but a sense of falseness.

How honest is the portrayal of various races and peoples? Do all of them resemble tinted Anglo-Saxons? What is the illustrator's feeling toward races other than his own? What appreciation of differences are we going to give our children? False generalizations about the goodness or evil of a race do little to create understanding.

Is the humor genuinely funny, or it is the tongue-in-cheek humor of the over-sophisticated adult?

How do the varieties of treatment reflect the sensibilities of the individual artist?

As we consider vitality we see how even more difficult it is to formulate any rules concerning this quality. Is there rhythm of line, of movement, of shape and mass in the drawings, and are these rhythms suitable to that of the story? If the text has sweep, do the pictures move likewise? Are the drawings so finished, so slick and photographically perfect that they were dead before we had a chance to look at them? This question is related to that of sensitivity of drawing. Do the drawings continue in the mind, . . . or are they so complete there is nothing for our minds and imaginations to do? Sheer virtuosity is often more useful in a juggler than in an artist. Is the drawing alive by itself on the page . . . or does it seem to live only because of its accurate resemblance to life?

... As we look at picture books we can find answers to all of these questions that will heighten our powers of discrimination. Perhaps the question that includes much of the foregoing could be — how rich is the experience in living the child gets, that I get, from looking at this book? ... Perhaps exposure to good picture books in childhood will not assure an adult taste capable of appreciating fine art, but I do believe that a child unconsciously

Then she saw some holes
to push the buttons through.

So that is what she did
with button one
and button two
and three.

12. Illustration by Ann Strugnell for *Sara and the Door* by Virginia Allen Jensen, Addison-Wesley, 1977, 5⅝ x 5¾.

forms an approach to his visual world of order, rhythm and interesting arrangements of color from the books he sees when young. The cleanness and simplicity of a well-designed page may start a chain of reactions that will continue into adulthood. If the child is accustomed to seeing varied and interesting shapes in his picture books, abstract art will not have the terrors for him that it seems to have for some adults. His discrimination, along with whatever of his individuality he can manage to preserve, will be his main defense against the bombardment of visual material on his eyes in most of his waking hours. . . .

Since art is a communication only in its own terms of line, color, and mass, we must learn to enjoy pictures with our senses instead of demanding logical explanations.

. . . In judging [books] I believe we should leave our personal prejudices for the illustrator or subject out of consideration. If an award is to be given to a distinguished book, let it be given to just that, the book that will carry the seal of . . . recognition

to the public. If a picture book does not wear well, can't we rightly ask ourselves was it ever really good, or merely timely? The book itself has not changed.

. . . Awards have an effect on the artists themselves. It has always been the fate of some artists to be either misjudged or to feel that their best work is unrecognized. Often an artist receives recognition for work inferior to what he has done previously. . . . Perhaps we have directly or indirectly asked these artists to repeat themselves. An illustrator must produce what sells in order to live. But to do his best work he must also be free to listen to his own inner voice and act upon it. Many illustrators are doing other art work as well as illustration in order to work in complete freedom. By buying only work that resembles an illustrator's earlier books we force him to stunt himself to our prescription. Let us encourage him to grow, to experiment, to try new techniques, by being at least receptive to the new.

The complete article from which these excerpts are taken appeared in *Illustrators of Children's Books: 1946-1956* (The Horn Book, Inc., 1958).

Bench Marks for Illustrators of Children's Books

by Warren Chappell

. . . Ernest Shepard, Sir John Tenniel, and A. B. Frost have managed in the *Pooh* books, *Alice*, and *Uncle Remus* to put their names as indelibly on these works as did the authors. They are like actors who have created roles and forever devised their stage business to their successors. It is interesting to note that all of them worked as professionals, drawing against weekly deadlines for periodicals. There is no hint of naiveté in their approach and no sign of any advisory intervention by a child psychiatrist. We must all regret that Stevenson and Mark Twain were not blessed with such perfect pictorial collaborators. From some of his comments it is evident that Mark Twain's graphic sense was

13, 14, 15. Illustrations by A. B. Frost from *The Favorite Uncle Remus* by Joel Chandler Harris, edited by George Van Santvoord and Archibald C. Coolidge, Houghton Mifflin, 1948.

not highly developed but he did know enough to be dissatisfied with his illustrators, and when Dan Beard was about to do drawings for the *Connecticut Yankee*, he wrote that he hoped Beard would read the book.

If we are going to call the children's book illustration of Shepard, Tenniel, and Frost ideal, in its way (and time has done just that), then we can learn a simple lesson: There should be no such category as children's illustration, for none of these men changed hats to undertake their celebrated drawings. We might then go even further and question the whole concept of illustration as something special and apart, rather than as a natural medium like painting or print-making. There have been more great artists who have been illustrators than not. And it is well to keep in mind that some of the greatest illustrations were not even made for publication, notably Rembrandt's for The Bible and Daumier's for *Don Quixote*, yet they are book illustrations.

Artists like Van Gogh and Picasso can be admired for their creations, and can stimulate and attract imitators, but they are sports and cannot teach. The bench marks of an illustrator would be sought in the works of those universal spirits who found so many of their themes in literature and who had what Baudelaire [in his book, *Eugene Delacroix, His Life and Work,* Lear Publishers, 1957] called "a kind of fierce spirit of competition with the written word." This was to describe Delacroix whose work, the poet observed, "sometimes seems to me a kind of remembrance of the greatness and passion of the universal man." One could hardly hope to find a better statement of what should be an illustrator's goal.

It should be taken for granted that an illustrator of books must know his craft. He should have not only a knowledge of the means of printing but a deep tactile sense of its capacities. He must be able to project his expression past the plate and the press and onto the sheet, for it is the printed result that is the end in view. Craftsmanship of the highest order will not make a great artist. It is the exception when menial engravers ascend the heights of art, as did Blake and Hogarth. Great artists, however, have always managed to be masters of the necessary craftsmanship.

"A classic must be about something and by somebody," said Carl Van Doren, in a short speech addressed to the subject "How to Write a Classic." This aphorism might just as well apply to artists as to writers, and it would be obviously absurd to expect a large bucket of imagination from a small well of experience. So an illustrator needs to know much more than the means of making drawings which will print. He should aspire to become a man of broad culture. Of necessity, his art must be his way of life, and his expression of life should be illuminated by his personal vision and his spirit.

In the days when artists learned through apprenticeship, a part of their training was to make copies from the large collection of drawings which were a part of the resources of every studio. Art was passed on, like an inheritance. But the beneficiary was in no way restricted; he made his own individual use of his legacy and in time passed it on, perhaps with some increase. For those illustrators who want to be a part of the continuity of exploration, to try to make their passage on the mainstream of art even though it might have to be along the shallower banks, it is still important to look at what has been done and to try to master it through understanding....

It is worse than hazardous to try to assemble a portfolio of drawings and prints for study by a mythical group of apprentices in a Universal Studio. But there are some artists who seem to

arrange themselves into a hierarchy of illustration and whose places there cannot be very hotly contested. Certainly their works contain essential bench marks for an illustrator. At the top I would put Rembrandt, "that sublime figure in the history of art." The lessons to be learned from Rembrandt are infinite, for his range of expression, as draughtsman, is so wide as to embrace almost the whole gamut of drawing. One looks in fascination at his simultaneous achieving of form and symbol, at his breathing, broken line that maintains the tension which is inherent in search. One can follow his inventiveness through a series of drawings on a single theme, as he moved around the subject like a painter moving around a model. Above all, there is a universal quality in his statements which lifts their themes above the level of incident. That is a prime objective for an illustrator, just as a portrait painter should want to achieve more than a likeness.

Below Rembrandt, put Daumier, Goya, Delacroix, and Callot, despite the fact that the last-named came before the first, in time, and had a great influence on him in both style and subject matter. For our purposes, especially, I would like to see Daumier lifted above the other three, for he was a professional illustrator and journalist and, like Rembrandt, he drew structurally and had the genius of fusing form and symbol....

It is the measure of Daumier's genius that, after a lifetime of illustration and journalistic drawing, he could turn to painting and do it with the same authority which had characterized his graphic work.

Goya is close to us in his draughtsmanship, and his violence is certainly not a stranger to our time. However, his chief messages to our mythical apprentices should lie in his boldly designed compositions and in his capacity to carry his passion past the plate and into a print.

Delacroix has been referred to earlier. . . . He was one of the giants of the nineteenth century and was a passionate reader of Shakespeare, Dante, Byron, and Ariosto. He was constantly taking themes from literature and his series of lithographs for *Faust* won Goethe's praise as being more than a complement to the text. One can learn from Delacroix because Delacroix spent his life in learning.

Callot is one of the most obvious ancestors of illustration as we know it. In him one sees the beginnings of several lines of illustration, especially the decorative, and above all he presages its eventual setting apart as a minor, and craft-aspect, of art.

In the drawings, paintings, and prints of these five artists any illustrator can find the nearest to absolute standards he should hope for. After all, perfection can only be achieved by the uninformed! Our apprentices must be searching for a broader understanding of the nature of drawing, its symbols and conventions, in all their varieties. They should want to see pictorial narration at its greatest, with incident providing the particularized setting for universal experiences. The making of a picture and the achieving of form are an artist's lifetime problems and he would do well to try to understand the searching improvisations and the constant efforts toward greater realization which were made by the masters. Perhaps then he might keep himself as dissatisfied as they were.

Of course, there are many other portfolios in the Universal Studio to which our apprentices have access, and in them will be the works of those who have made particular contributions to illustration. Among them are the revelations of Blake, the social commentary of Hogarth and Gavarni, the caricatures of Rowlandson and Busch, the historical reconstructions of Menzel, the illustrations made for children by Caldecott, Tenniel, Frost, Lear, and Nicholson, and the exuberant drawings of Doré.

I wish to conclude with a quotation from Boardman Robinson, a great draughtsman and illustrator and my dear friend and teacher:

"The practice of illustration, as I see it, is in one respect quite different from easel or mural painting, for it necessarily refers to something outside itself. The subject matter, the literary content, assumes a new significance, and the illustration must reflect this. From my point of view, the illustrator would not enter upon his task with too fixed a preconception; he should not have in mind too pronounced a pattern. The illustration is not pre-composed, but it must be allowed to grow, so to speak, from the seed of the impulse. Upon reading a poem or a work of fiction or history, I *see* a picture, and I go to work, usually without sketches, and I try to bring the picture to life, to develop and make actual that subjective impression. This subjective impression is, by definition, my own, not the author's, although he provides the stimulus. My impression is not his, nor is it that of any other reader." [1]

16. Illustration by Edward Lear from *The Complete Nonsense of Edward Lear* collected and introduced by Holbrook Jackson, Dover, 1951.

There was an old man of Port Grigor,
Whose actions were noted for vigour;
He stood on his head, till his waistcoat turned red,
That eclectic old man of Port Grigor.

1 Albert Christ-Janer, *Boardman Robinson*, Chicago, University of Chicago Press, 1946.
Excerpts from the article which appeared in *The Horn Book Magazine*, October 1957.

Contemporary Art and Children's Book Illustration

by Leonard Weisgard

The subject of this discussion is contemporary art and its influence upon illustration in books for children; yet who can translate a visual art into a verbal tone? We would do better to take hands and walk around the world at a comfortable pace and actually see what the creative genius of the artist has to offer today, what has gone before, and allow for what is still to come. We would do better still if, in our walk, we could look at these creations with the fresh eyes of a child, the heart of an adult, and the mind of a mature being.

Certain general conclusions would be obvious from such observation.

Art is not art unless it distills sensation and spirit, re-presenting them with enhanced means and in memorable form.

Art is miraculously precise and communicative.

Art has the power to instruct without words; it engenders an intuitive knowledge of life that no other medium is capable of; and it extends the meaning of life by the representation of simulated and ordered experiences.

The means whereby art accomplishes these ends are shaped by judgment and discipline; and the development of judgment and discipline is a lifetime learning process.

In any age, the artist is representative of his time and environment. He will either work within their philosophical concepts or rebel against them. Artists are human beings. They dream similar dreams, but, like all of us, they react differently to similar truths. In the world of art today there are artists who seek to preserve the ageless principles of humanism. There are also those who strive to express their struggles with twentieth-century mechanical determinism.

The latter, and the world, have been victimized by the scientific age. The world has ceased to cultivate aesthetic sensibilities in its younger generations: the artist, therefore, tends to abandon artistic traditions since there are few to appreciate or understand them . . .

Discontent with the older established ways of artistic expression appeared early in the nineteenth

17. Illustration by Leonard Baskin for *Moon-Whales and Other Moon Poems* by Ted Hughes, Viking, 1976.

Leonard Weisgard was awarded the Caldecott Medal in 1947 for his illustration of The Little Island *by Golden MacDonald (Margaret Wise Brown). His books have also received awards from the American Institute of Graphic Arts and the Society of Illustrators. He has lectured on art and on children's books at many colleges and schools. The basis for this article was a talk given by Weisgard at a Conference on "A Study of Eye Appeal in Children's Books," held at Pratt Institute, Brooklyn, in 1959.*

century. This paralleled a similar discontent with the use of words; in poetry, drama, and novels, words were manipulated to break structure and release form, to express sensation not thought, to be inarticulate not communicative. Jacques Barzun, in *The House of Intellect*, says that the revulsion from words, syntax, and coherence accounts for the widespread anarchy in the handling of language as well as for the preference for the abnormal in our conception of the real.

Discontent with the older established ways of artistic expression also paralleled the psychological concept of that period that the mind in its most secret operations was an unconscious artist.

Subsequent findings in our day have turned art still further away from the intellect, directing it instead to exploring the depths of unconscious imagery and creating forms void of all known associations. Meaning has evaporated, because clear thought is no longer considered an important constitutent of art. Perhaps, in a world of anguish, abstract presentation is a legitimate tool of expression; but, alas, we have not yet evolved a system to clarify the private world of symbols — alike as they may be, throughout all of man's time — whether they be created by writer or by artist.

Many painters today feel that the camera has taken the place of the scientific and realistic representation of the Renaissance painters. It is interesting, however, to observe the photographer also breaking away from the realistic, catching instead an *emotional* response with a humanistically sympathetic lens. Such a photographer is Henri Cartier-Bresson.

To return, for a moment, to the early part of the nineteenth century: it was the Impressionists who first broke away from the Academic. They evolved new color formulas and a less realistic approach. Cézanne, Gauguin, and Van Gogh cast aside the Academic viewpoint and, using the colors of the Impressionists, emphasized structure and composition in their paintings. In their paintings, too, was the personal expression of each, surging forth in paint.

The search for new ways of expression continues among contemporary artists. Matisse exemplifies the leadership of France in this search. He simpli-

fies forms and expresses them with an Oriental influence of line, using brilliant flat colors. Matisse also denies Western perspective and evokes a kinship with early Egyptian and Cretan murals. Matisse and Picasso were interested in primitive African art, and distortions such as those seen in African masks appear in many modern paintings.

So does modern art reveal influences from all parts of the world, from all times, as it does now from the realm of science. The contemporary artist cannot escape these influences in this age of easy communication and good reproduction.

A shift in taste has been gathering momentum for three generations. From the Symbolist period on, Western art has been based on the repudiation of what is common — common speech, common knowledge, common life — and its replacement by the singular and indefinable.

And now comes a transition to a noisy emphasis on design. It is not our purpose to fathom here the reason for such a transition, or to question the rights of artists to do as they see fit. The effect of the transition is in no doubt: art has never been so quick and potent in its influence, nor has design, be it for good or bad, ever been so strenuously bandied about, for any and all purposes.

These, then, are some of the factors pulling at modern art today: the distrust of nature; the bewilderment at changing standards of beauty as fostered by certain critics; and the struggle between the intelligible and the unintelligible. Repercussions of these phenomena in modern art appear even in books for children.

Illustration in many children's books today is infected by the abstract elements in painting: the artist attempts, self-consciously, to achieve the level of accomplishment that the unself-conscious child attains, naturally and artlessly. Unless the artist has a special genius based on sound draughtsmanship, he cannot easily achieve honest and joyous communication with another human of *any* age. It is not so simple as just drawing or painting as a child does.

Let us look now into some of the healthy influences modern art has had on books for children. The rigid rules and regulations that governed art and design in children's books yesterday have vanished.

18. Illustration by Nicole Rubel for *Sleepy Ronald* by Jack Gantos, Houghton Mifflin, 1976, 9⅛ x 8¾.

19. Illustration by Beverly Brodsky McDermott for *The Crystal Apple* adapted and illustrated by Beverly Brodsky McDermott, Viking, 1974, 8⅝ x 7½.

the ships on the River Volga—
even a sturgeon,
asleep in a deep pool.

So has the marmalade school of sentimentality and over-decoration. A boldness and vitality are at such healthy play today that I wonder sometimes why the vigor of the art work does not grab the book and run off and away with its content.

Modern art impulses, plus a reinvestigation of folk-art motifs, have vigorously benefited the Middle European countries which are swinging forward again the production of children's books. Twenty years ago European picture books were generally far beyond ours, but lately, except for the instance named, some of their products appear to be suffering from many of our unhappier mistakes.

The strongest and healthiest influence on children's books from modern art comes from the use of color. There is little need to dwell on the potent use of color to heighten emotional response in illustration, so well does color speak for itself.

Perhaps we should pay brief respect to the dramatic use of space as another direct influence from modern art on children's book illustration as well as on architecture, sculpture, and other forms of graphic representation. Mondrian's abstractions and designs have had an enormous impact upon illustration, layout, furniture design, and contemporary building structure.

The infatuation-with-texture group of illustrators is an interesting tangent of modern art. The artists would seem to be rebelling against solidity, almost returning to animal tactile instincts.

Modern art has had a profound impact upon the kind of illustrating and painting that is being done for film work, television, and commercial advertising. Perhaps it is ironic that these three media periodically raid the children's book field for fresh artists — grist for their mills.

It is exciting and remarkable to ponder upon these threads of artistic communication that link us all together, to discover there are designs of this extraordinary universe still to be explored, and to realize that the separation of cultural and artistic worlds is a growing impossibility. . . .

Excerpts from the article which appeared in *The Horn Book Magazine*, April 1960.

The High Art of Illustration

by Lee Kingman

A rather esoteric argument has been going on for years as to whether or not illustration is legitimately called art, or, as it is sometimes qualified, high art. Certainly illustration is an art form. It is a graphic art. It is a commercial career.

But since the days of the illuminated Books of Hours, an illustrator has never been accorded the same kind of recognition and respect as a painter or a sculptor by the academicians, the patrons of art, or the buying public. . . . This attitude is still reflected in some art schools, in the election of artists to national academies, and in financial returns to illustrators.

Milton Glaser, well-known artist and winner of the Gold Medal of the American Institute of Graphic Arts in 1972, pointed out [that]: "the essential function of art is to change or intensify one's perception of reality. Through most of history perception and information existed simultaneously in works of art. . . . As society developed, the information and the art function diverged, and distinctions were made between high art and communicating information to increasing numbers of people. High art, of course, is supposed to have the more elevating characteristics." [1]

As defined in *The American Heritage Dictionary of the English Language*, illustration is "visual matter used to clarify or decorate a text." But going far beyond clarification, many illustrations do indeed accomplish the essential function of art: *to change or intensify one's perception of reality*: and thereby to produce a lasting effect on the beholder.

[1] Milton Glaser, *Milton Glaser: Graphic Design*, Woodstock, N.Y. The Overlook Press, 1973.

In other words, illustration can perform that originally unsophisticated achievement of allowing heightened perception and information to coexist in a work of art.

Hearing the title of a book, which might have been read years before, can cause a vivid instant replay of a particular picture — even before the characters and the story come into focus. Take N. C. Wyeth's painting of the formidable seaman, Billy Bones, done for the famous Scribner edition of *Treasure Island*. Coming upon it in a gallery of paintings, wouldn't you be caught by the intensity of the man and the bleak atmosphere? It has the same piratical stance seen in many portraits of princes and doges. Or upon seeing the picture of Blind Pew groping along a road against a black sky with faint stars — a questing figure with a mysterious blindfold and foreshortened shadow from the moonlight — wouldn't you think it a surrealist painting? The forceful imprint of these illustrations stays in the memory, and their impact derives as much from their quality as paintings as from their literary inspiration.

... [I]n his way Leo Lionni has used collage as effectively as Matisse. Ellen Raskin has turned calligraphic [and typographic] cartwheels even more effectively than Robert Indiana, with his famous four-letter word, LOVE. William Pène du Bois's trees are as innocently haunting an environment as Rousseau's jungle, and his koala bears stare as daringly as Rousseau's animals. John Steptoe's slashing black outlines have Rouault's authority, but with the added vitality of movement. Nancy Ekholm Burkert's dwarfs are as commanding of reaction on the viewer's part as those painted by Velázquez. But because such achievements are presented within the structure of a book, they go without [the same] recognition as high art.

... Alphabet books have existed for several hundred years. ... There is [an extreme contrast between nineteenth-century] Kate Greenaway's *A Apple Pie* [and today's *Hosie's Alphabet* with its exciting paintings by Leonard Baskin.] ... [T]here will always be those who feel more at ease with Greenaway's tidy children and gentle animals than with Baskin's "bumptious baboon" with its haunting blue eyes, his arrogant "carrion crow," or even his poignant "sweet-throated nightingale at dusk." But both Greenaway and Baskin call for some kind of subjective reaction, some conscious act of reception or rejection on the part of the viewer, and this process of constant choice is what makes particular illustrations memorable or consigns them to ... oblivion.

... Yet is it really because a picture arises from a text that we label it illustration? Aren't some of the great paintings in the entire history of art illustrations of Biblical stories and historic events, from Leonardo da Vinci's *Last Supper* to Picasso's *Guernica*? Surely the content of a picture, as well as the way it is done, cannot help but creep into the elusive distinction made ... between a work of high art and an illustration.

The recognition of the picture's content as part of its quality, so that perception and information exit simultaneously, is once again taking on more than aesthetic importance.

Glaser also says: "Now we're beginning to realize that all aspects of communication, whatever the form, have extraordinary implications to the community receiving the information. And so we can't afford not to pay attention to the quality of information that is distributed. In fact, we know that a comic strip may have a more profound effect on its community than a work of Picasso. ... In other words, it's important to have a critical view of these artifacts because they are so terribly significant in establishing the mythology and the ethos of a people." [2]

Glaser's statement that we must pay attention to the quality of information being distributed emphasizes that the time has come to recognize the illustrator as a significant artist whose work has a long-range import. [Where] the comic strip, the photographic essay, and the filmstrip (the whole gamut of audio-visual material now flooding into the marketplace) are just becoming part of our culture, illustration already has an established place.

So we view our classic illustrators, whose works have endured for generations, with an even keener eye. What brings continuing pleasure in the work of Caldecott, who so explicitly portrays everything

---

2 Glaser, *Milton Glaser: Graphic Design.*

THEN MICKEY IN DOUGH WAS JUST ON HIS WAY

20. Illustration by Maurice Sendak for *In the Night Kitchen* written and illustrated by Maurice Sendak, Harper, 1970, 8½ x 11.

21. Illustration by Leo Lionni for *Alexander and the Wind-Up Mouse* written and illustrated by Leo Lionni, Pantheon, 1969, 8⅝ x 10¾.

That very afternoon Alexander went into the garden and ran to the end of the path. "Lizard, lizard," he whispered. And suddenly there stood before him, full of the colors of flowers and butterflies, a large lizard. "Is it true that you could change me into a wind-up mouse?" asked Alexander in a quivering voice.

"When the moon is round," said the lizard, "bring me a purple pebble."

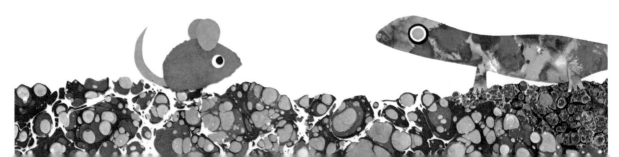

22. Illustration by Leonard Baskin
for *Hosie's Alphabet* by Hosea,
Tobias and Lisa Baskin, Viking,
1972, 7¾ x 11½.

23. Illustration by William Pène du Bois for *Bear Circus*, Viking, 1971, 7⅞ x 10⅞.

from John Gilpin clinging to his horse — to sheep huddled against the wind? It is his strong line and spirited drawing. Why should Kate Greenaway survive, with her improbably clean children? Because, despite their idealized garments and faces, they provide a feeling of nostalgic genre, of a time and place that might have existed, if only because it was transmitted by an artist who believed in it so thoroughly. Who needs Maxfield Parrish? Those who like mystery and richness and incredibility in their *Arabian Nights*. ([A] contemporary artist who handles colors with such vibrancy is Brian Wildsmith, although his brashness is in complete contrast to Parrish's tight style.) Who wants Howard Pyle? Those who enjoy the stylized strength of his pictures with their vigorous figures, and the crispness and drama of his composition. The extravagance and decoration used by Kay Nielsen in 1912 for *The Twelve Dancing Princesses and Other Fairy Tales* seemed uncomfortable during periods when realism and naturalism took over. But now the fantasy in Nielsen's illustration is being enjoyed

again, and perhaps there will also be a revival of books illustrated by Edmund Dulac. We can never replace Rackham. No stage production or film of *A Midsummer Night's Dream* that I have ever seen has equaled the provocative enchantment of Rackham's ethereally weird wood, filled with creatures of delicacy, humor, and plain asininity.

Some of our contemporary artists who have paced their own work and given wholly of their perceptions and inner resources are producing the classics of the future. Each of us already has his favorite Sendak, whether it be *The Light Princess* or *The Juniper Tree and Other Stories* or *Higglety Pigglety Pop!* His uncompromisingly vivid work, as shown in *Where the Wild Things Are* and *In the Night Kitchen* gives the reader "total experiences" — to borrow a bit of jargon from the high art world.

. . . [W]hether one enjoys the visual explosions of Etienne Delessert and Tomi Ungerer (both of whom can border on the outrageous at times) or the more subtle inner vision expressed with humor in the work of William Steig, Edward Gorey, Beni Montressor, John Burningham, Margot Zemach, and Arnold Lobel, does depend largely on one's personal reactions.

. . . It is much harder now to pick out specific illustrations that may grow to the stature of high art than it was in the period 1900 to 1930. Artists today are too seldom given the time to develop, to bring to their work the qualities which will make it enduring, and to create illustrations that will attain the rank of high art.

Excerpts from the article which appeared in the Fiftieth Anniversary issue of *The Horn Book Magazine*, October 1974.

24. Illustration by Maurice Sendak for *The Juniper Tree and Other Tales from Grimm,* selected by Lore Segal and Maurice Sendak, Farrar, 1973.

II

Notes About Artists and By Artists About Their Work

25. *The Doryman* by N. C. Wyeth. Copyright © 1938 by N. C. Wyeth. Reproduced by courtesy of Mrs. Norman B. Woolworth.

N. C. Wyeth (1882-1945)

by Dudley Lunt

When tragedy stalked in the valley of Brandywine and sudden death dropped its hand on Wyeth's broad shoulder, it was children everywhere who suffered the greatest loss.[1] For forty years in a steady flow illustration after illustration . . . had been the product of his brush and palette. His record is written in bold outline and glowing color with the classics of children's literature . . . and to this will come the children of the future to absorb without conscious effort, as is a child's immemorial way, this product of a lifetime rich in vital action and wide experience.

The first thing about Convers Wyeth was a paradoxical characteristic. Bold and adventurous, he never for a moment sat inert physically or mentally. Yet his capacity for absorption of the moment and the locale was developed to a most remarkable degree. Born in the lee of Boston in the winding valley of the Charles River at Needham, he left these parts when a boy. Yet to the end of his life he retained with all the freshness of youthful impression his early exposure to the Massachusetts countryside. Then in the richness and with the mastery of a lifetime's experience he portrayed it in *Men of Concord*. . . . In point of ancestry he was of Yankee stock on the one hand . . . and on the other his mother was Swiss.

. . . Young Wyeth soon headed toward the west. He was sixteen. He towered over six feet. And he was on his own. In the half decade that lay ahead . . . he coupled formal instruction at art schools with an adventurous trip in the west. There he drove stage-coaches, lived on Indian Reservations, became a cowpuncher, ran an Indian trading post and herded sheep. He was a privileged participant in the great American adventure and tradition of the western plains.

This virile and earthy life was soon reflected in his life's work. Indeed his first publication — Wyeth could write and write well, as well as paint — appeared in March, 1906, in *Scribner's Magazine* under the title, "A Day with the Round Up." In his six illustrations of cowboys, cattle and horses are to be seen the vivid and explosive action, the fidelity to truth in detail and the lyrical quality which distinguishes his later work. . . .

To the end he bore upon him the indelible imprint of these impressionable years. . . .

The valley of the Brandywine had welcomed Wyeth when he was just of age. Here in the rolling hills . . . he studied, struggled, and worked in the early years — painted, taught and wrote, married, built his home and studio on the side of a hill overlooking the valley to Chadds Ford, brought up his children and growing ever — died. Here, in short, he fashioned his own mark as man and artist.

It was with the school of Howard Pyle that he was first identified. The desire to study under this master had brought him to Wilmington in 1904. His formal schooling had been that of a New England youngster in a small town, coupled with instruction at the art schools available in Boston and with C. W. Reed, an artist there. From Howard Pyle he derived in diverse aspects. There were, of course, the mystery and technicality of craft. Then there was his exposure to the master's devotion to the American colonial tradition and to that of the Middle Ages. Lastly and indubitably the most important, there was sympathetic contact with a remarkable teacher of great human understanding and an artist of integrity and noble ideals. While the impress made was strong and the benefit derived was great, it is a very great mistake indeed to identify Convers Wyeth with any school of art at all. He was destined, and in short order he did start, to stake out his own claim to greatness. . . .

---

[1] On October 19, 1945, three days prior to his sixty-third birthday, Newell Convers Wyeth and his three-year-old grandson namesake were killed together in a railroad crossing accident near his home at Chadds Ford, Pennsylvania.

Dudley Lunt, a lawyer and long-time friend of the Wyeth family, has written several articles on the so-called "Brandywine Tradition," considering the careers of Pyle and of N. C. Wyeth.

... [A]s the New Englander uses the word, Convers Wyeth was an *able* man. By which there is meant to be conveyed that a man himself has perfected a kind of ability, distinctive and wholly his own, so that if another attempts to employ it, that other is perforce an imitator.

There is a remark of Thoreau's that he was fond of quoting. It was to the effect that the action of doing a thing and the writing about it should be so close that they amount to one and the same thing. This, he would maintain, is precisely true of painting.

Coupled within him with this thought was his advice to the young illustrator that "his salvation lies within himself [and] that to be able to draw virile pictures means that he must live virilely." In the joining of these conceptions in his own life is the key to his art.

Thus it was that he could plunge into a tale and historical research and so capture their spirit that in his pictures it was as if he himself were at once onlooker and participant. The famous illustrations of *Treasure Island* — Jim Hawkins "led like a dancing bear" by Long John Silver, the buccaneers storming the stockade, the fight in the mizzenshrouds and cross-trees and the rest, evoked a letter in praise of their authenticity from R.L.S. himself. The mere mention of others will bring one's favorites to mind — *Kidnapped* and *David Balfour*, the Leather-stocking tales, *Deerslayer* and *The Last of the Mohicans*, *Robinson Crusoe*, *The Mysterious Island*, *Westward Ho*, *The Oregon Trail*, *The Odyssey* and the *Bounty Trilogy*. . . .

Throughout his life the bulk of Wyeth's work was in oils. In the last decade, consistent with his never ceasing growth, he made himself the master of a technique which, albeit it was an ancient one, was entirely new to him. This was the use of egg tempera on gesso panels. And as Paul Horgan has well said, "In Tempera he found a new clarity and crispness." The man's extraordinarily receptive reaction to the earth and life about him made a vivid response in a new vein that was rich and luminous and clear.

The State of Maine had by this time become as much a part of him as had . . . the rolling valley of the Brandywine. At Port Clyde on the vast reaches of the Atlantic he had a summer home within range of the beacons of Monhegan and Matinicus. Here are the Maine Folk and the scenes so superbly pictured in what is undoubtedly his most characteristic and representative work in the field of illustration — *Trending into Maine*, written by his friend Kenneth Roberts. Here he had ample scope for the historical depiction in which he had always excelled. Here again are New Englanders, his own folk, reminiscent of the *Men of Concord*. There is the old fisherman in his dory at sunset. In Wyeth's words . . . the old timer was "settin' his dory 'crost the cove." In the picture of the lobsterman hauling his pots off a spruce-crowned headland, Wyeth has caught the somber and lonely feeling of fog in a way that is unparalleled in all the annals of American art.

In sharp contrast of scene and character are his illustrations for *The Yearling*. With characteristic thoroughness he visited the cracker country of Florida as he had the Carolinas when, a dozen and more years before, he had illustrated *Drums*. Here he tramped the country up and down talking to the people and listening to their tales until there accrued, within the receptive recesses of his nature, their very essence to be later distilled in his pictures. If you do not believe this, look into the eyes of the three Forrester brothers as they ride to town through the pine scrub atop a wagonload of moonshine and quarreling bear cubs.

It is curiously interesting and indeed significant that the peak of Convers Wyeth's work in the field of illustration is to be found in a book wholly devoid of fiction, narration and action. I refer again to the excerpts from Thoreau's Journals in *Men of Concord*. The reason lies at the core of the man after half a century's experience in living. Here he had full scope for his expression of his sheer joy in the simple, the familiar and the commonplace things in life. As he grew in power throughout his lifetime, so, I venture to suggest, this quality of his art is destined to have its own growing and timeless appeal both in this field and with his paintings of this later period.

Excerpts from the article which appeared in *The Horn Book Magazine*, September-October 1946.

My Goals as an Illustrator

by Marcia Brown

. . . It might be useful for me to tell you of my work on three different books, each of which presented a different problem in illustration and bookmaking. . . . One is a picture book, one a picture-story book, and one an illustrated book for older children. All three are of folk origin: one is a fable, one of the oldest types of folk tales; one is a synthesis of several European folk tales through a

Marcia Brown has twice been awarded the Caldecott Medal, given annually since 1938 by the American Library Association for "the most distinguished picture book." In 1962 she won the medal for Once a Mouse, *and in 1965 for* Cinderella.

poet's mind; one is a hero legend with chants from a people with an oral culture.

Myths and legends tell a child who he is in the family of man. In a book with ancient mythic origins, some of the poetic depth of the story should be implied in the illustrations. The child, looking and reading, will understand and recall tomorrow more than he can tell you today.

Once a Mouse is a picture book in which the pictures complete a very brief text, and, I hope, add some comment of their own. Since the book is for very young children, the details are only those needed. The woodcut is a favorite medium of mine, one that relates to traditional graphic media and that can be very successfully combined with type on a page.

Though the words of the fable are few, the theme is big. It takes a certain amount of force to cut a wooden plank, and a definite decision. Wood that lived can say something about life in a forest. An artist can make his own color proofs in printer's inks, can mix his colors and give approximate formula to a printer. Even though the transparent colors on an offset press are different from the thicker ones used at home, this proving can be of enormous help in seeing what one will get.

26. Illustration by Marcia Brown for *Backbone of the King* written and illustrated by Marcia Brown, Scribner, 1966.

Each artist has his personal feeling about his way of working, and the finished book is what is to be judged as successful or not, but in my own books I like every color to be cut on a separate block in order to maintain the optical unity of the medium. A book is like a very small stage. Just as a violent drama on television is sometimes hard to take in one's living room, what is effective in a large print can often break up a comparatively small book page.

The story of *Once a Mouse* moves in an arc from quietness to quietness; from meditation, to concern, to involvement, to anger and action, back to meditation. The colors I chose were the yellow-green of sun through leaves, of earth, the dark green of shadows, and the red that says India to me. Red is used as a force to cut into the other colors when its violence is needed. Excitements are fairly easy to make in illustrations — a chase, a fight, an explosion — and offer immediate release. The quiet power of inner life is much harder to achieve and must be felt more deeply.

In the fall of 1962 I was invited to go to Hawaii as guest of the Honolulu Book Fair. Just before I went, I had reread *The Wild Swans* of Andersen. Hawaii made a great impression on me. But when I flew from one island to another, the shadow of the plane on the clouds below reminded me of Elisa in her net borne by her wild swan brothers. When . . . I saw the huge waves crashing in at Sunset Beach, I thought of the endless rolling waves that gave her courage to be inexhaustible in her search for her brothers. There are vast images in that story, vast implications and sonorities that can ring in a child's mind far into adult life. It is a story of light and shade, with strong contrasts: dark toads that turn into bright poppies when they touch Elisa; the forest pool in its shadow and the shimmer of light through the leaves; the darkest part of the forest that is also the deepest despair. . . . And then the free, vast spaces of the sea, the dark waves rearing up to show their white sides.

A white swan swoops down over the dark vault of Elisa's prison; between the black cypresses that would be there in an Italian graveyard shines the

27. Illustration by Marcia Brown for *Once a Mouse . . . A Fable Cut in Wood* adapted and illustrated by Marcia Brown, Scribner, 1961, 8⅞ x 9½.

changed the cat into a big dog. Not long after that, a hungry tiger

The night was very dark; not a single little glowworm shone out of the moss, and with a troubled mind she lay down to sleep; and then she thought that the branches above her parted and Our Lord looked down on her with loving eyes, and the little angels peeped out above His head and beneath His arms.

When she woke in the morning she was not sure whether she had dreamt it or whether it really had happened.

30

28. Illustration by Marcia Brown for *The Wild Swans* by Hans Christian Andersen, Scribner, 1963, 7 x 9⅞.

moon. Over the dark tumbrel the eleven swans descend with a great flashing and beating of their white wings, and the story ends with the miracle of the white flower, like a star blooming on the pile of faggots, and the dazzle of light and happiness.

To try to show these contrasts I used a broad lettering pen dragged over rough water-color paper and sumi for the gray washes. I needed the simplest means of achieving dark and light. The rose color for the swans' beaks, for the dawn, for the poppies and the roses I got from rubbing sanguine powder into the plastic contact plate. I was afraid to trust delicate washes either to drop-out half tone or hand-clearing. The drawings were frequently vignetted around the type to tie the two more intimately together and to give variety to the movement of the book.

. . . While I was writing the story of Paka'a [*Backbone of the King*] which swings back and forth from the delineation of character to the natural phenomena that form character and provide images of magnificence to describe it, I was naturally thinking of the illustrations. Full color would not only have been out of the question in cost for a long book for older children but would have intruded too insistently on a story that is one of internal struggle and growth as well as external action.

Except for enigmatical pictographs, of great interest to anthropologists but very primitive graphically, and wood and stone images of gods, there was almost no Hawaiian art that seemed effective to me as inspiration for illustrations for a legend for young people with probably a vague picture of a tourist's paradise. I had thought of a carved

35

29. Illustration by Marcia Brown for *Backbone of the King,* Scribner, 1966.

medium, woodcut or linoleum, one that might hark back to the elegantly simple carvings and also one that could depict the atmosphere in which such legends arose. I finally settled on linoleum, and two points of view evolved in the illustrations that are also in my telling of the story. One is the background of vast natural forces — the winds that were thought to bear the tales; the basalt cliffs that gave an ideal to men's character; the vast spaces of the sea, source of life and food, testing ground of prowess, image of both beauty and poignant and unfulfilled longing. The other is a simple delineation of character, pared down to its essence in the most direct of emotional confrontations. Linoleum, which can be cut or engraved, seemed to be the answer.

The color I chose for the printing was close to that I recall most strongly when I think of Hawaii — the deep green of the clefts in the great palis, where all softness has worn away in the wind and rain but where living plants have clad the cliffs in velvet. I chose a deep, warm, almost olive green to harmonize with the warm-toned paper.

Margaret Evans, who designed the typography, chose Palatino, a type that has the strength and individuality in its cut to halt the eye on the individual word. I had tried to tell the story with strong, simple words, most of them Anglo-Saxon, words of action, with metaphors taken from Hawaiian life. The pictures would have to reflect the feelings of those words. Big things had to remain big. Action should have meaning, but thought and inner feeling are also action in illustration. I found this illustration for older children a challenge, with a more rigid type page than that of the picture book, with a very different mental approach from the reader.

The title page is symbolic — the steering paddle that meant command; the kahili, the feather standard, that meant royalty and the watchful care of a backbone for his king; the cliff that meant the rock-heart that does not yield or wear away. A windy book from a windy land.

In *The Little Prince,* Saint-Exupéry makes a statement in the context of one human relationship that perhaps we could apply to another: "One is forever responsible for whom one has tamed." Children walk, arms open, to embrace what we give them. To hand on to them the breakdown in communication that is all around us is a very serious thing. Those who work with children should be encouraged to hand on to them their personal involvement with the world. A child needs the stimulus of books that are focused on individuality in personality and character if he is to find his own. A child is individual; a book is individual. Each should be served according to its needs.

Excerpts from the article which appeared in *The Horn Book Magazine,* June 1967.

30. Illustration by Randolph Caldecott for *The House That Jack Built,* Routledge, 1878.

Caldecott's Pictures in Motion

by Hilda van Stockum

Few artists have achieved so much in so short a time as Randolph Caldecott. Perhaps he felt that he would not live long, for his work matured surprisingly fast. When he illustrated Washington Irving's *Old Christmas* and *Bracebridge Hall,* he was still influenced by the style of the period with its intricate shading. We have to know him well to recognize his hand in those pictures. . . . It is, however, to Caldecott's Picture Books that I am confining this paper — those books which I knew and loved as a child — as this gives me the advantage of two points of view, one of the past, the other of the present. Thinking of those early years, made bright by Walter Crane, Kate Greenaway, Tenniel, Leslie Brooke, Beatrix Potter, Elsa Beskow, Willebeek Le Mair and, of course, Caldecott, I notice a peculiar thing. Whereas the other artists have all left me a legacy of definite, stationary pictures which I can pull out of the cupboard of my mind and examine at leisure — the goose that WAS a goose, Peter Rabbit entangled in a net, Alice swimming in her tears — I don't remember any particular picture of Caldecott's. But at the sound of his name, as to the tune of a Pied Piper, a procession of little figures comes dancing past — horses with red-coated riders, shaggy dogs, loving couples, children, kings, queens, dishes, and a cow jumping over a moon. So I have come to the conclusion that Caldecott provided me with my first movies.

Randolph Caldecott (1846-1886) was the English artist for whom the Caldecott Medal was named. This medal has been given annually since 1938 by the American Library Association to "the most distinguished picture book" published in America in the previous year.

When leafing through his Picture Books, it is this ebb and flow of perpetual motion which strikes one first. Other artists like to dwell on the scenes they are creating, either from contemplative joy in their beauty or from a psychological joy in their social values. Not so Caldecott. He is always aiming at the next picture; his very figures seem to be pointing to it; one cannot wait to turn the page and see what happens next.

As an artist, I am interested to see how Caldecott achieves this effect of continuous movement. I think he does it through a lavish use of horizons; his people are either coming at you, large as life, or vanishing over a hill. You can never be sure of them; now they're here, now they're gone. There lies the great contrast with Leslie Brooke, who belongs to the "Come-gather-around-and-I'll-tell-you-a-story" kind of drawing. One has a sense of living in Johnny Crow's Garden; but if one day John Gilpin should fail to slow down and leaped headlong from the white cliffs of Dover, no one would feel surprised.

It is this vigorous action which endears Caldecott to children, who don't look at pictures to admire, but to participate. As a daughter of mine put it, they want to be "in the book."

The next characteristic of Caldecott's work seems to me to be its joyousness. When I had grown up, and hadn't looked at my old Picture Books for a long time, I happened to pick up one day *The Three Jovial Huntsmen* . . . the most typically Caldecott of all his books. It is the one that comes first to mind. And it is also the most English of his books, with its Pickwickian characters. It starts off with that lovely house — doesn't it speak of early morning tea, roaring fires, plum pudding and punch? The joviality of the huntsmen is apparent right away, when the middle one salutes the sparrows. It is obvious he has nothing on his mind, has a good digestion, and is prepared to find anything on God's earth entertaining. They are kind huntsmen, too; they pity the poor scarecrow, cheering him up, for he strains after them rapturously as they careen away again over several more pages. They are like small boys, detached and happy, examining everything they meet. Next, it is a stupid old grindlestone who becomes so enamored of them that it pursues them to the indignation of the farmer and his wife and their scandalized house.

31, 32. Illustrations by Randolph Caldecott for *The Three Jovial Huntsmen,* Rutledge, 1880.

No wonder the huntsmen are exhausted after all that. The reader can rest for a moment as they mop their brows and allow their horses to drink. But soon they are off again, greeting a calf who responds to their merry mood as do the children, who wouldn't be children if they didn't. The pig, however, in the nakedness of his complacency, scares the huntsmen back into the open where one of them promptly comes to grief, showing the proper use of his horn. Meanwhile Mr. Caldecott shows us the proper use of the pen, drawing with a few strokes a drama in the distance: the other huntsmen discover their loss and, veering around, lead back the riderless steed.

Finally they come to the climax of their trip and frighten a loving couple out of their wits like the bad boys they are. Then back again to their comfortable house as the sun goes down. One senses the healthy glow of the hunters in the still evening light, and their complete love for one another. Here is all the exuberance and consolation of childhood. And one feels one has made the trip oneself and leans back to rest a while.

Let us take two versions of *John Gilpin* — the one illustrated by Caldecott, the other done a little later

by Charles E. Brock. It is obvious that Mr. Brock has seen Caldecott's work and admired it. His characters have a strong resemblance to Caldecott's, even to the details of clothing. Otherwise the style is quite different. Mr. Brock makes precious, shaded pictures, very beautiful in themselves but not suited to the spirit of the poem. . . . There is such a shining finish of detail that the story limps with it, whereas one races through Caldecott's with a flicker of pages. Also, Caldecott gives his scenery a generous share in the action, while Mr. Brock's backgrounds could be moved from one picture to another without affecting the story at all.

This participation of nature in Caldecott's pictures is seen, for instance, in the colored picture where John Gilpin tries to turn his horse around. Here the swallows dance madly about in the air, the donkey brays dismally, and the distant houses prick up their chimneys. Even when Mr. Caldecott's houses are indifferent they are purposely so; they seem to be saying "I'm only a house, I'm not in on this; you can't expect it of me." Whereas Mr. Brock's houses aren't saying anything, but seem to have strayed out of a book on "how to draw houses in correct light and shade."

33. Illustration by Randolph Caldecott for *The Great Panjandrum Himself,* Routledge, 1885.

. . . Every artist knows how easy it is to be led away from the main theme through interest in some detail; to enjoy drawing a tree, a horse, a gown, and forget the action . . . But Caldecott always sacrifices the lesser for the greater. If one line can do it, no two lines are used. Nor is he in love with line itself, as is that incomparable graphic artist, that creator of line lyrics, Mr. Darley. With Caldecott, the story is supreme. Even the grass on the ground adds to the general effect — either waving wildly or twinkling with merry little dots or regarding itself peacefully in a pond. When the "man all tattered and torn" in *The House that Jack Built* leads away "the maiden all forlorn" the daisies bow respectfully before the Power of Love.

One could go on . . . endlessly, enjoying story after story with all its silent byplay: Mr. Panjandrum actually explained; nursery rhymes receiving proper endings in the pictures, if not in the words; minor characters getting tacitly their due. Every-

where the same candid simplicity; no display of artistic fireworks, no pomposity, no evasion. Like a child, Mr. Caldecott goes to each work he illustrates, taking in all the meaning and all the ramifications of meaning and unstintingly bringing out each point. He is like his own jovial huntsmen — no creature is too mean for his attention, his affection, and his humor. And always everywhere, this tremendous vitality and love of life in all its forms. How meager would be our knowledge of England, how many pictures poorer, without this great draughtsman who makes his country live for us — the ditches, the fields, the thin snow, the cottages, the towns and the wonderful ladies! Where else but in England can one find ladies and gentlemen at the drop of a hat?

So let us take off our hats to that deftest of all gentlemen, that humorist, that artist, that friend — RANDOLPH CALDECOTT.

Excerpts from the article which appeared in *The Horn Book Magazine,* March-April 1946.

Illustrating
The Wind
in the Willows

by Ernest H. Shepard

"There are certain books that should never be illustrated" is true in many senses, and I had felt that *The Wind in the Willows* was one of these. Perhaps if it had not already been done, I should not have given way to the desire to do it myself, but it so happened that when the opportunity was offered me, I seized upon it gladly.

The characters that Kenneth Grahame chose for his story — the little animals from the woods, the fields, and the waters of England — and which he portrayed with such sympathy and understanding showed, to me, how clearly he had seen into the mind of a child. Indeed, they had grown from the letters and stories he used to write from time to time to amuse his own child.

Mother Earth has a lot to offer to those who try to understand her and to know the ways of the little people who live, who burrow, who scratch, and store, and who climb and swim; whose short lives are spent in the hunt for a livelihood, be it worms or beetles, nuts or fish. Like us human folk they are forever busy — Mole, the field worker, the digger; Rat, the perfect waterman, wise about currents, eddies and what not; Badger, big and stout, uncouth but oh! how dependable, a champion of the smaller folk; and Toad, the impossible and lovable,

Ernest H. Shepard, English artist (1879-1976), needs no introduction to those who know Winnie-the-Pooh, Piglet, Eeyore, and Christopher Robin. His illustrations for Kenneth Grahame's books, however, are also justly famous.

never out of a scrape and never ceasing to boast. These are not caricatures, they are the real thing, brought to life by a man who loved them and all that they stand for, and it was he who told me where they lived and where to find them.

Kenneth Grahame was an old man when I went to see him. Not sure about this new illustrator of his book, he listened patiently while I told him what I hoped to do. Then he said, "I love these little people, be kind to them." Just that; but sitting forward in his chair, resting upon the arms, his fine handsome head turned aside, looking like some ancient Viking, warming, he told me of the river near by, of the meadows where Mole broke ground that spring morning, of the banks where Rat had his house, of the pools where Otter hid, and of Wild Wood way up on the hill above the river, a fearsome place but for the sanctuary of Badger's home and of Toad Hall. He would like, he said, to go with me to show me the river bank that he knew so well, ". . . but now I cannot walk so far and you must find your way alone."

So I left him and, guided by his instructions, I spent a happy autumn afternoon with my sketch book. It was easy to imagine it all, sitting by the river bank or following the wake of little bubbles that told me that Rat was not far away. Across the water lay the flat meadows and somewhere there I

34, 35. Illustrations by Ernest H. Shepard for *The Wind in the Willows* by Kenneth Grahame, Scribner, 1953.

knew that Mole was, even now, making ready his bed for the winter, to wait for the first breath of spring — and again beyond, on the rising ground, the great expanse of Wild Wood with Badger laying in his winter stores. Toad, I imagined, would be snoring in post-prandial ease in his armchair away down stream at Toad Hall. I poked and pried along the river bank to find where was Rat's boat house, and where Mole had crossed the water to join him, and, as I listened to the river noises, the little plops and ripples that mean so much to the small people, I could almost fancy that I could see a tiny boat pulled up among the reeds.

Dusk was settling, down on the water, with a rising mist, but, above, the late sun was shining on the wood — a faint afterglow of autumn glory, when I turned homewards, treading carefully just in case something was underfoot.

I was to meet Kenneth Grahame once again. I went to his home and was able to show him some of the results of my work. Though critical, he seemed pleased and, chuckling, said, "I'm glad you've made them real." We seemed to share a secret pleasure in knowing that the pictures were of the river spots where the little people lived.

This is the story that I can tell of how it came about that I was to play my part in helping to bring *The Wind in the Willows* a little nearer to the reader. If I had not met Kenneth Grahame I should never have had the temerity to embark on the work, but he gave me encouragement that no one else could have given me, and I wish that he could have lived to see the finished work, whatever his verdict would have been.

One more word — way down the river, on the hill beyond Marlow, among the lovely woods, is the home where the bells of Marlow Church come pealing across the valley, and where, on a winter's night, strange little footprints might be seen on the snow — funny little hoofprints meandering, perhaps unsteadily. Could it be Bertie and his friends, I wonder?

From *The Horn Book Magazine*, April 1954.

Wanda Gág, Fellow-worker

by Rose Dobbs

What was it like to work with Wanda Gág? Memories crowd upon memories. "Author" as a general descriptive term never quite applied to her. What she contributed to our relationship and the manner in which she made that contribution went far beyond any contractual obligation. Early in our careers we became friends and so dispensed altogether with both "author" and "editor." Then Wanda went a step beyond friendship. She found a word, fellow-worker, which she liked and which she used generously.

As I look back, I realize that Wanda found the perfect word to describe herself. In every sense she was always the fellow-worker, never the omnipotent writer or temperamental artist. That is why she got along so well with other workers. She had her ideas and convictions, certainly. Was she not a superb craftsman with the craftsman's high standards, insistence upon attention to the smallest detail, and pride in a good job well done, whether by herself or by someone else? But she also had understanding, which made her at all times respect the limitations imposed upon any craft; and sympathy, which made her at all times willing to recognize the difficulties other workers faced; and humor, which many a time saved an "incident" from becoming a "tragedy."

In the beginning, especially with printers, there were many problems. It was a constant affair of

---

Rose Dobbs was the children's book editor at Coward-McCann, with whom Wanda Gág was working on More Tales from Grimm *at the time of her death in 1946. The entire May-June 1947 issue of* The Horn Book Magazine *was published "in tribute to Wanda Gág."*

give and take, teach and learn. Richard Van Rees, Jr., puts its this way: "She educated us, and we educated her. She knew what she wanted, but she was always willing to listen; she was never unfair, and she was *fun*." One of the things Wanda felt the printer needed to be educated about was the matter of black ink. Pigs may be pigs, but black is not always black. Black, to Wanda, meant *color*, the rich, sparkling color of the blacks in her beautiful prints and lithographs. It took a good deal of insisting on her part, administered with much charm, to teach the printer what she considered to be black. She, on the other hand, had to learn that commercial printing was not fine limited-edition printing; that imperfections will appear in the very best grade of paper, thereby affecting the printing; that the printer's business was heir to many unpredictable mechanical ills for which he, poor wretch, could not always be held responsible. Yes, they educated each other — and me. It was a happy day for Wanda when the printer told her that other customers were asking for "Wanda Gág black ink," and a happier day for the printer when she reached the point where she could say: "You know how I want it; it isn't necessary for me to come down."

. . . Memories . . . Wanda acting as if she came from Missouri instead of Minnesota, insisting gently but firmly upon revise after revise of engraver's proofs until even her sharp bright eye could detect no flaw. "A hundred per cent isn't possible," the perspiring engraver would say. "Besides, see, this is only a speck." With an engaging smile and a twinkle in her eye, Wanda would answer: "Perhaps not a hundred per cent, but surely ninety-nine?" And she'd explain to me: "If we let this go through, true it's only a speck and hardly noticeable in this one proof, but by the time the edition is run it will have become an ugly blot. No, you must never okay an engraver's proof unless it is okay and the only way you can tell is to see for yourself."

. . . Memories. . . . [T]he vast unlimited realm of type, uncharted territory to both of us. Wanda would say: "I only know how I want the finished page to look. With these small sturdy peasant drawings, the type shouldn't be pretty; it should be solid and round and sturdy, like a peasant, if you

36. Illustration by Wanda Gág, for *Tales from Grimm* freely translated and illustrated by Wanda Gág, Coward, 1936.

know what I mean, and of the same weight as the pictures. If the type is too light it will look as if it doesn't belong on the page, and if it is too heavy it will push the pictures right off the page. It must be just right so that the type and pictures together make a complete illustration which fits nicely into the margins." On another occasion she said: "Don't you think the type should assume a slight air of elegance, in deference to all the princes and princesses in the stories?" Nor was the appearance of type her sole concern. There was the matter of ease in reading. She spent much time over the sample pages of *Tales from Grimm* after she had approved the type wondering why she was still un-satisfied. Then, after consulting with children, she put her finger on the trouble. The fairy-tale age had dropped since she was a child; eight- and ten-year-

olds instead of twelve- and fourteen-year-olds were reading fairy tales. Few children of eight to ten read with great ease; for one thing they were being taught to read "by words." Type, even large type, set in its regular measure seldom permitted *enough* space between the words, creating a definite handi-cap for the child reader. Couldn't she, Wanda asked, see still another sample page with more space between the words? Try an experiment sometime. Give an eight- or ten-year-old Wanda's *Grimm* and any other edition and ask the child to read to you. It will prove an eye-opener.

Excerpts from the article which appeared in *The Horn Book Maga-zine*, May-June, 1947.

Virginia Lee Burton's Dynamic Sense of Design

by Lee Kingman

When Virginia Lee Burton created her final book, *Life Story*, published in 1962, she was in total command of her ability to combine design, illustration, and text in a manner distinctively her own. But the student of illustration, book production, or design, can learn much by seeing how she developed her theories from the time her first book, *Choo Choo*, was published in 1935.

At that time Virginia Lee Burton lived in [Folly Cove] on Cape Ann [in Massachusetts]. When her first son, Aristides, was old enough to be intrigued with the sounds of trains, his mother was just as fascinated with their shapes and their energy. The strong black-and-white patterns of the trains racing across the pages of *Choo Choo* are bursting with motion. Choo Choo never waits placidly . . . the engine always looks ready to spring out along the track.

This sense of movement, whether derived from the action inherent in an illustration, or from the changes and contrasts in a design, is an essential quality in all Virginia Lee Burton's work. She studied art at the California School of Fine Arts in San Francisco; she also studied ballet. . . . Her love for and appreciation of dancing was an important part of her whole life. . . .

Lee Kingman studied design with Virginia Lee Burton, founder and teacher of the Folly Cove Designers, and became a member of the guild-type group of craftsmen who for thirty years designed and block-printed textiles and maintained a famous shop on Cape Ann, Massachusetts.

To one so kinesthetically motivated as Jinnee, drawing must have seemed an extension of dance, the capture of motion on paper. But another vital element in her work, the clarity of her drawing, certainly came from her study with her husband, George Demetrios, one of the few great teachers of life drawing.

. . . Given these two qualities, the exuberant sense of movement and the clear ability to depict it, Jinnee had to find a way to hold them down on a page. With her second book, *Mike Mulligan and His Steam Shovel* (1939), she . . . use [d] the double-spread pages as a unit and . . . place [d] the lines of text in a specially shaped area. She felt that the illustrator should be allowed by the publisher to command all the elements on the page — the type and unit of text as well as the pictures. . . .

Mike Mulligan was written for her second son, Michael . . . and the sturdy blond little boy racing up to see the arrival of Mike Mulligan and Mary Anne in Popperville was definitely drawn from life. There is a relaxed freedom in this book, even though the vitality of its many figures depends upon the organization of each page, an indication of things to come in her later work. . . .

In 1941, Jinnee was distressed by the influence of comic strips and comic books on children. She deplored the bad drawing and meaningless themes, and took great delight in offering her boys a substitute, *Calico the Wonder Horse or the Saga of Stewy Stinker*. Whether she would have cared to admit it or not, the comic strip format of squared-off sequences influenced the development of her design techniques in *Calico*. . . . [O]ne of its delights is its end papers . . . [which] tell a lot about Virginia Lee Burton's methods of working. They show the complete design of the whole book in quick sketches of the action appearing in the black-and-white pattern of each page. Of course, almost every artist works out a dummy before beginning any finished illustration. But Jinnee always lived in the middle of hers. Once the dummy was made, up went the sketches for each page, tacked in sequence around the studio, gradually replaced by "finished" illustrations still in sequence. One of her habits . . . was constant visual criticism of that segment of work by itself and in relation to anything before it or after it. Suddenly looking up, she might

He had seen Stewy Stinker and his gang of Bad Men . . . Butch Bones, Snake Eye Pyezon, Buzzard Bates and little Skunk Skeeter . . . in the Badlands. Stewy Stinker was said to be so mean he would hold up Santa Claus on Christmas Eve if he had a chance. He rode a horse whose name was Mud.

see, in a page supposedly completed days ago, an area or a line she knew needed changing. To do one book, she filled wastebaskets full of what other artists might well have considered completely satisfactory work. . . .

The illustrations for *Calico* were done in black-and-white on scratchboard, the perfect medium for an artist who keeps enriching and changing the black-and-white areas as the illustration emerges. A black line in a white area can be eliminated by scraping it off the surface. A white line in a black area can be easily incised. Black dots are penned for tone and texture, or white dots cut out of the black. Compared to the precise and exquisite work Virginia Lee Burton did for *Song of Robin Hood* six years later, *Calico* is an early stage in both her design and her use of the medium. But the quick-

ness and dash of the illustration excitingly carries out the comic strip feeling she obviously used and transcended. The double spread on pages 6 and 7 of *Calico* carries a continuing flow of design, yet it is a good example of how each illustration can stand alone. Even the distant cattle are contributing to the motion of the whole as they stand in swirling loops that grow in size. After the subject of her designs or illustrations — here the cowboys — the next important element in her design theory was called "sizes." The contrast in size of the subject — the cowboys and horses being larger on the left-hand page than they are seen in perspective on the right-hand page — helps to build a sense of motion. The third important element of her design was "tones" — the black, white, and gray areas being used, in this case to emphasize each other. . . .

They looked down on Cactus County where there were no fences, no locks and no jail, not even a Deputy Sheriff. They saw the nice fat cattle grazing peacefully on the open range.

'Ahaa!' said Stewy Stinker as he curled his long black moustache. 'Ahaa!' said he. 'Nice pickin's!'

37, 38. Illustrations by Virginia Lee Burton for *Calico the Wonder Horse or The Saga of Stewy Stinker* written and illustrated by Virginia Lee Burton, Houghton Mifflin, 8⅜ x 5¾. The artist completely redrew the illustrations for this 1950 edition, which replaced the earlier 1941 edition printed on wartime poor-quality paper.

... With *The Little House*, the Caldecott Medal winner published in 1942, Virginia Lee Burton's name was permanently established in children's literature.... In the book Jinnee made her Little House small and simple and gave her a traditional shape, to emphasize her survival through decades of change. But the country setting, as seen in the cycle of the seasons, is very close to the appearance of the Demetrios' [house and] yard.

Jinnee was strongly influenced by her physical surroundings and . . . [s]ince nature is omnipresent, yet ever-changing, she apparently felt no limiting sense of repetition in using the theme of small home and changing seasons more than once

— [*Life Story* recapitulates some of *The Little House* in its last twenty pages.]
... While I was an editor at Houghton Mifflin, she was working on *Katy and the Big Snow* (1943). Snowblowers were news then and I remember her making a rush trip from Gloucester in a snowstorm to sketch . . . a snowblower [as it penetrated] the streets of Boston, even though the new machine never appeared in her book. She had merely convinced herself that Katy, with her shiny, shapely V-plow, made a much better heroine than a fussy, sputtering snowblower ever could.
. . . The book on which I worked with her closely was *Song of Robin Hood*, published in 1947 after

39. Illustration by Virginia Lee Burton for *Song of Robin Hood* selected and edited by Anne Malcolmson, Houghton Miflllin, 1947, 9 x 11.

three years of study and drawing on Jinnee's part. [It contained] Anne Malcolmson's edited selection of the Robin Hood ballads and [Grace Castagnetta's] . . . piano accompaniments for the melodies. . . . The format emerged slowly, although the full-page illustrations announcing each ballad were part of the scheme from the beginning. Also there was usually space at the end of each ballad for another drawing. But what bothered everyone was the stiffness and awkward spacing of the short four-lined stanzas sharply bisecting each page. Jinnee had been studying the old manuscripts illumined by the monks, and her study inspired her to illustrate every single verse, a method which would not only balance the area of text on each page with pictures, but would bring out the action in the ballads. Even though Jinnee set herself an appalling schedule of arising at dawn . . . and working till evening . . . this infinitely detailed illustration of over four hundred verses added a whole year to the preparation of the book.

. . . "Robin Hood and the Ranger" is a particularly good example of how she made her design theories work for her. . . . Robin, arms outstretched in open defiance, argues his right to shoot a deer to feed his merry men. The forester gestures his protection of the deer, for they are the King's. The deer are already in flight. In many illustrations the gestures of the men and the running of the deer would be the extent of the action. But this whole illustration is full of movement, and the design helps to bring this about. The wood violets are springing up all over the forest; it is Jinnee's careful control of the size of the flowers and the density with which they grow which keeps this area of the picture from being simply background, underpinnings, or useless decoration. Although only a few trees are used, their swirling arrangement creates the feeling of deep forest. Birds, rushing out of the trees, add to the disturbing sense of confrontation; changes in their size emphasize the sense of flying up and away. The sun . . . is indeed the Phoebus of the ballad, with its rays not just decorative effect, but seeming to shoot the spring sunshine into the forest.

Many of the Folly Cove Design exercises were based on how to turn a "black" to a "white" through a "dark grey," a "medium gray" (half-and-half) to a "light gray." To achieve this thoroughly . . . took time, infinite patience, a steady hand, and a learning eye. . . . [U]sing this one illustration as an example of the possibilities, consider the leaves on the tree at the very center of the picture. This [area] is more white than black; thus, a light gray tone. The trees in the middle of each side are a medium tone; the trees at the edge, where black dominates through the white leaves, are a dark gray. Thus the texture and tones of the forest have not stood still to the eye. On the forest floor, the same range of tone is carried out in the wood violets, starting at the left with a black tone and going through medium gray at the left of Robin's foot, to the dark gray behind him, with a highlight of very light gray between the feet of the two men. . . .

With *The Emperor's New Clothes* (1949), Jinnee turned again to color. The story was one she had liked as a child . . . and the theme of the parade, panoply, and elegance was fun to treat with design and embellishment. She retold the story so she could control the length of the text and make the type area on each page an integral part of the whole design.

In 1952 *Maybelle the Cable Car* brought her tribute to San Francisco and expressed her delight in the cable cars. The book was credited with helping to preserve the famous cars. . . .

The study for *Life Story* and the painstaking painting of the full-color originals absorbed eight years of Virginia Lee Burton's life and was exhausting to her, physically and creatively. . . . She was not in the best of health during her last five years [but s]he had a strong New England conscience. What else could have driven her to the years of early rising and the extremely long days of work on her books? But like any disciplined artist, she accepted the necessity of boring routine and infinite detail to make what she did perfect, and she had little patience with anyone's work that she felt too quick, too unfinished, or imitative. . . . As she could not do another book, it is appropriate that *Life Story* was her final, all-encompassing creation.

Excerpts from two articles which appeared in the October and December 1970 issues of *The Horn Book Magazine*.

The Artist and
His Editor

by Grace Allen Hogarth

40. Illustration by Barbara Cooney for *A White Heron* by Sarah Orne Jewett, Crowell, 1963, 6⅛ x 9¼.

... When a picture book artist is struggling with an author's unmanageable manuscript, the editor who is responsible for the end product is often tempted to ask the author to cut his text or rewrite it with pictures in mind. This is, however, dangerous ground. All reviewers have a deep reverence for the written word. When Barbara Cooney cut the text of *A White Heron* so that it could become a picture book, she made a work of art that I am certain Sarah Orne Jewett would have loved. But the book was received with a storm of protest in the United States. Even in England, where the author was not widely known, Margery Fisher wrote in *Growing Point*: "The text has been cut and edited, for the most part discreetly. I hope I shan't seem pernickety if I say I wish more of the author's beautifully shaped sentences had been left untouched.... The more leisurely style of the last century is valuable in its own right and a joy to anyone reading aloud. I believe children who delight in words will respond to this finely wrought but very human story. There is no doubt that this edition will attract them for its open print and fine layout and for the incomparable colored illustrations." [1]

To this the editor can only say that if the long sentences had been left there would not have been room for any "incomparable colored illustrations." The editor's decision is, perhaps, a larger one. Is the material wrong, or right, for a picture book?

1 Margery Fisher, *Growing Point*, July 1964.

At various times in her long career in the field of children's literature, Grace Allen Hogarth has been artist, author, and editor of the children's book departments of major publishing houses on both sides of the Atlantic.

. . . An artist's interpretation and the power of his brush or pen must inevitably mark the author's work with the imprint of another mind and another personality. There is a striking example of this in the American and British illustrations for *Le Hibou et la Poussiquette,* Francis Steegmuller's translation into French of *The Owl and the Pussy-cat* by Edward Lear. In the American edition, Barbara Cooney made the rhyme into a light-hearted picture book in a squarish shape that would delight young children as well as adults and make them laugh. She used color — turquoise for sea, yellow that is true *citron,* and shades of green from grass to olive. Monique-Alika Watteau, who decorated the English edition, chose a tall thin book and made sophisticated black-and-white designs rather than realistic illustrations. Her book is more serious and more adult. By studying these two editions of the same translation of Lear, one can see how easily the visual image as described by the author can be interpreted altogether differently by different artists. The editor who chooses the

illustrator has, then, a responsibility as serious as that of accepting the manuscript for publication.

. . . It is true that the marriage of author and illustrator is not often made in heaven, but I have come to believe that the editor must try to make this marriage work. The best books are not always those in which a rarely gifted writer draws his own pictures, but those in which an illustrator, working in harmony with an author, enriches the written word and adds a new and valid dimension. A successful collaboration is worth many failures, and the give and take can be mutually rewarding.

William Stobbs, another winner of the Kate Greenaway Medal, has many times worked successfully with his authors. If he makes a hilly background when it should have been flat, he cheerfully levels it down. Nevertheless, when he once appeared on a platform as part of a Brains Trust team that included an author who confessed that she had several times altered her text to suit a slightly inaccu-

41. Illustration by Barbara Cooney for *Le Hibou et la Poussiquette,* French text by Francis Steegmuller, Little Brown, 1961.

42. Illustration by Monique-Alika Watteau for *Le Hibou et la Poussiquette,* French text by Francis Steegmuller, Rupert Hart-Davis, 1961.

rate illustration, he was seen to leap to his feet, crying, "Let me embrace you!"

In the gentler world of 1865 when *Alice's Adventures in Wonderland* first made its appearance, the author was able to express his views on the "defective" printing, a matter in which he was most scrupulous. At his insistence the majority of the first issue was withdrawn. It is unthinkable today that an author or artist could achieve the rejection of a printing job. Fortunately, however, an editor can, and sometimes does; but he is hampered by the sad fact that his public is largely uncritical and will often accept without comment books that should be rejected. A reviewer may possibly spot defective printing, but a good story, even with unreadable type and poor illustrations, will sell. Without the support of his customers, the editor's case is weakened and unless the printing is bad enough to scream aloud, author and illustrator must suffer.

. . . It is interesting that one of the first picture books printed by photolithography [in the United States] was . . . *Little Tim and the Brave Sea Captain* [with pictures by Edward Ardizzone]. The four basic color plates were on metal thin enough to wrap around cylinders which, one at a time, as they turned, printed each color onto a rubber cylinder which, in its turn, printed the image onto the paper. This gave an even softer effect than if printed directly onto the paper and allowed the image to be front-to on the plate since it was reversed on the rubber and printed right way round on the paper.

. . . The first edition of *Little Tim* was printed in New York in the summer of 1935 and had the rough passage of all pioneers. In particular, the ink failed to dry because it was very hot and very damp; the paper expanded and then contracted, making the register of one color on the next uncertain, and there were all kinds of minor technical hitches. The final result was a large sixty-four-page book, carrying the color on thirty-two of these pages with blanks in between. This was not intended, but was the result of the drying problem.

A milestone had been passed and a discovery made about the printing of picture books. Why then did they not at once pour forth in a stream from the new presses? The answer is a simple one: cost. . . .

In the United States the clever editors persuaded their illustrators to do the work of camera and retoucher by making their own separations for each color. Sometimes an artist was paid an additional fee for making his own color separations, but often a royalty covered both the work of separating out the colors and the original art work. This labor of the artist greatly cut production costs. Indeed color might not have been possible at all if the artist hadn't learned to cooperate in this way. The result was quite like the old lithography from stone, and, since the work was done by hand, shading was obtained by softening the line, often by crayon strokes, and not, at first, by a mechanical screen. The development of this craft of color separation by American artists from the mid-thirties to the present day is a fascinating chapter in printing and publishing history. As the artist's skill developed, the printer's skill also improved until it was possible to produce an almost flawless result in, for example, *A White Heron* with Barbara Cooney's illustrations. Her earlier color separations had, for the most part, been simply line drawings with areas of solid color, as in *Chanticleer and the Fox* and *The Little Juggler*. Her separations for *A White Heron*, however, were given a wash effect which she obtained by tying chamois leather over her brush. The printer faithfully reproduced each delicately shaded separation by using a screen in the making of his plates. . . .

Excerpts from an article which appeared in *Illustrators of Children's Books: 1957-1966*.

Jane Jordan said she wanted to live in the country so she could go swimming and catch butterflies and have a pony to ride.

Jimmy Jordan said he wanted to climb trees, and have a dog, and go fishing, and hunt in the woods.

The more they talked about it the more they all wanted to live in the country. But Mr. Jordan had to keep on working in the city until he had enough

money saved up to buy a farm and move to the country.

When Mr. Jordan finally had enough money saved up, he still didn't know what kind of a farm to buy. So they decided to take a trip and look at some farms. Then they packed up their bags and locked up their apartment, and all got in the car and drove off across the country to visit the ten biggest farms they could find.

43. Illustration by Dahlov Ipcar for *Ten Big Farms* written and illustrated by Dahlov Ipcar, Knopf, 1958, 9⅞ x 8.

Making Pictures on the Farm

by Dahlov Ipcar

... I love farm life, even though it is hard work. I think I will always feel romantic about it. There is visual beauty all around me. Color and pattern are everywhere. Haycocks and windrows form designs in the fields. Plowed fields are beautiful with the shine of light along the furrows, and the plow teams in yellow blankets with red stripes. I love the browns and grays of the cows in the whitewashed barn. They seem to me as beautiful as antelopes. Even the clothes that the men wear are as bright

Dahlov Ipcar attended progressive schools in New York City, but never had formal training in art. Her parents, William and Marguerite Zorach, were both artists who preferred to let her absorb the creative activities continually going on around her, without even instruction from them. She has painted murals, had one-person shows in New York, and several of her paintings have been acquired by the Whitney and Metropolitan museums.

reds and greens as you would find in any medieval miniature. I didn't always live on a farm; I was brought up in New York City. I think perhaps I first decided that I wanted to live on a farm when I was only three years old. So never underestimate how early a child's life plan is formed....

... It took me fifteen years to realize my aim. Finally, when I was eighteen, I managed to marry a nice young struggling accountant, and persuade him to try farm life. I was very lucky, because if he had been a happy accountant I would probably still be living in the city. But he didn't like city life, either, and he makes a fine dairy farmer.

You might ask whether I also decided at three to become an artist. I don't think I ever decided that; it was just as natural a part of my life as breathing. It never occurred to me that anyone might live a life without art. Both my parents were artists, and our home was always full of artistic activities. It was really a house of wonders. My mother was busy making batiks, embroidering bedspreads and clothes for us, hooking rugs, and, of course, painting pictures. Our walls were painted with murals of the Garden of Eden; and every piece of furniture — mostly discards from the city streets — was painted in gay colors. My father was busy carving in one room, but he could take time out to make me a costume for Hallowe'en, all covered with moons and stars and blazing suns of genuine gold leaf.

My parents gave me no formal art training. They both felt that their own art had been hampered and misdirected by the academic training they had received — they were among the first of the modern art movement — and they wanted to see what would happen if a child's art were to develop as naturally as possible. They gave me a great deal of encouragement, and they took me to visit museums and artists' studios and showed me the best in art. Most important of all, my father taught me about integrity. He taught me that an artist must never create art to sell. If he does, it won't be Art. He must work because he has a tremendous urge to create; he must put his heart and soul into his work and do the very best he can. Then, only after the work is finished, should he try to sell it. My father also warned me against commercial art. "Never get involved in it," he warned. "They'll tell you what to do; they'll pester the life out of you. You won't be able to call your soul your own!"

You may well wonder how, after all this, I ever came to be illustrating children's books. Fortunately, I have never had to compromise. No one has told me how to do my pictures. I have done children's books because I loved doing them. I have enjoyed all the work involved. And I don't have to sell them; the publisher does that. The only thing I have to sell is the idea, or the text, for by some strange and, to my mind, backward process, it is the story that is bought, not the pictures. I write the stories too, but only as a sort of excuse for doing the pictures. I'm afraid I think as an artist, not as a writer; I think in terms of pictures. I think of something I would like to paint, and I write a story to go with it.

But I feel a picture book, even for very young children, needs some valid idea. It must convey some message or point of view, reveal some truth about the world, or awaken some new interest in the things around us. I have a million and one ideas for pictures, but I only get about one idea a year for stories. . . .

I have been able to do all my books and all the art work on them through the mail. I find that this gives me time to think problems through and work them out, and I am not so dependent on other people. Often I write my editor or my production manager about a problem, and by the time they reply I have solved it myself. I should think this would be rather frustrating to the editors, but they seem happy. I feel that an editor's function is not to tell us how to write or paint, but to prod us into doing our best. Sometimes a word of criticism is very helpful. When I first submitted my book *Brown Cow Farm,* I had planned it as a counting book from one to ten. But picture books come in standard sizes, and thirty-six pages is about the shortest. Even using double spreads for each number, ten numbers only take up twenty pages; so I padded it with a little story front and back. Peggy Lesser, of Doubleday, said, "We like this, but it isn't either counting book or farm story. Can't you

44. Illustration by Dahlov Ipcar for *Black and White* written and illustrated by Dahlov Ipcar, Knopf, 1963, 7⅝ x 9⅞.

Black-and-white zebras and antelopes graze   Through the long, hot jungle days.

do something about it?" I wanted to keep it a counting book, but I couldn't see how to work it out. Then early one morning, about four o'clock (I always get all my best ideas at four in the morning), it came to me. Why not make this a real counting book and have it develop by tens to one hundred? All children are thrilled when they discover that once you have learned to count by tens you can count to any number, even one thousand or a million. . . .

My dinosaur book, *The Wonderful Egg*, also came from memories of my own childhood, in this case from my early love of prehistoric animals. When I was seven I painted a frieze of them all around my room. My own sons were fascinated by dinosaurs, too, and begged me to paint dinosaur pictures for them. I even made them dinosaur Easter eggs. We were a little ahead of the rest of the world, but now other children seem to have caught up with us, and they all share our interest in dinosaurs. One of the things that amused me in the reviews of this book was that some reviewers, while praising it as "quite scientific," took exception to the "unscientific color." Of course, no one knows what color dinosaurs were, and I see no reason to imagine that they were ugly putty-colored monsters, so I made them as gay in color as possible. Small reptiles are often beautifully and excitingly colored, and it seems possible that the big ones might have been also.

Other books of mine such as *One Horse Farm* and *Ten Big Farms* are drawn directly from my farm experience, and *World Full of Horses* from my love of the old-fashioned way of life that we lived when we first came to Maine. *I Like Animals* expresses, of course, my own lifelong interest in every kind of animal life.

My books and my art sometimes overlap. I seem to draw ideas from each for the other. I love to paint animals more than anything else, and because I can visualize them so clearly in my mind's eye I am never dependent on models. I can show them in action as one could never capture them even with patience and a camera. My art is fairly close to nature, but not dependent on nature. I am free to do anything I choose. If I paint the things around me it is only because I find them more strange and exciting than fanciful things. But I am never earthbound; if I want to do fantastic things I can, because even the real, everyday things I paint are all done from my imagination.

I am a firm believer in inspiration. The mind is an amazing storehouse. While mine may have a limited supply of textual material, there seems to be no end of the pictures that are stored there. I sometimes feel that I am troubled with visions; I see so many marvelous pictures when I close my eyes. They arise without any conscious effort, a multitude of completely new and beautiful designs and things I have never seen or imagined. I have seen Mexican fiestas in my mind's eye, complete with gorgeous and fantastic costumes in astounding colors. Everything is very elusive; patterns and colors change swiftly as in a kaleidoscope. I remember recently doing a painting of a snake winding down a tree, and I must have seen a hundred snakes winding down a hundred different trees, each with a different and equally beautiful change of color and design.

In general I would say that my art is a happy art. A great many artists these days are afraid of cheerful pictures. They want to be taken "seriously" and nothing insures this better than painting pictures that drip gloom and despair. This pretentious tragic posing is as ludicrous in its way as the heavy-handed Victorian attempts at pathos and melancholy.

Perhaps I lead too happy and healthy an existence, but I much prefer to convey the beauty and excitement of simple everyday life. There is an infinite, incredible mystery in beauty. Everything living is beautifully designed. Each animal has a distinct form and personality and life of its own.

I like to do art for children because I feel they love these living things as I do. They love each animal and leaf and look at it with wonder. People ask me how I manage to find my way back to the world of childhood, and I say that I am still a child at heart. Perhaps I am not really; perhaps no one can remain a child, even deep in his heart. But for me the sense of wonder is still there.

Excerpts from the article which appeared in *The Horn Book Magazine*, October 1961.

Artist's Choice

The articles which follow are selected from a series, "Artist's Choice," inaugurated by Ruth Hill Viguers when she was editor of The Horn Book Magazine. *They appeared intermittently from 1950 to 1962. Mrs. Viguers felt, and these comments show, that artists often have a different way of looking at pictures and are very articulate in sharing what to them is important about illustration.*

BERTIE'S ESCAPADE written by Kenneth Grahame

Illustrated by Ernest H. Shepard

Comment by Louis Slobodkin

The chaos that whirls through contemporary art has even now fluttered a few pages in children's books. In the 1949-1950 season there were drawings by the students of the great modern masters. Others were done in the styles (imitative and diluted) of the great modern masters. But there were no drawings by the modern masters themselves. Fortunately, we do have one book by a master draughtsman, Kenneth Grahame's *Bertie's Escapade* with its sparkling drawings by Ernest H. Shepard.

To my way of thinking (and I claim no originality for these thoughts) an illustration in a children's book should open windows in the pages of a book; it should serve to let in light. It should get beyond the surface of the paper and dig deep to create space — boundless space. It should raise

45. Illustration by Ernest H. Shepard for *Bertie's Escapade* by Kenneth Grahame, Lippincott, 1949, 5½ x 7⅜.

(or suggest) full-bodied, luminous form. It should extend the lyric flow and unify the mood and emotional concept of the script. If it does not do these things, it is not an illustration for a children's book. It belongs in a book for adults.

I do not claim Shepard's drawings in *Bertie's Escapade* have all the elements I hope to see in illustrations. Rather he tends to achieve them. His style is built on years of solid development; it is completely woven into his consciousness. And although his style is built on long tradition, it is his own.

Shepard is a communicative artist. His drawing is not for the precious few; it is for the many. There is no attempt to distill line or form or space to its very essense. Pure gold needs some gross earthy alloy to give it body and substance. Perhaps it's because of this earthy alloy ever present in Shepard's art that I turn to his drawings with so much pleasure.

Is Shepard modern or old-fashioned? (Not that the children who love his work care — but just for argument's sake, "Is he?") The newest and very dewiest quality a piece of modern art should have, I have been told, must be a "humanistic quality."

Is there anything warmer or more 'humanistic'' than the drawing I've chosen for this article? Here Bertie, Peter and Benjie (sleepy and cold) find themselves propelled suddenly up into Spring Lane in front of Mr. Stone's lodge. They plan to sing carols, etc.

Have you ever seen Donatello's large-bottomed infants tottering and rocking on their tiny feet? Or the dancing cherubs on the pulpit in Florence or the angels making music in Padua or that Cupid wearing pants in the Florence Museum? This drawing of Bertie, Peter and Benjie made me think of them when I first saw it. It may seem pretty far-fetched to find the elements of Donatello in this little drawing. But aside from his handling of the masses of the main figures, look at the whirling indications on the wall that have so good a tone relation to the rest of the drawing. Mr. Donatello often used such devices in his reliefs. And another relation — there's nothing soft or sweety-sweet in Shepard's drawings of these stout-bottomed little beasts — there's nothing cuddlesome. Donatello rarely produced cuddlesome babies — even those who sat on the Madonnas' laps were real infants.

Donatello and Shepard in his own way preach crisp forminess. Now that we've already taken up Bertie and his friends and the way they stand in space on the snow, — what of the snow, the snow-sprinkled bushes, the knobby wall? Everything takes its place and function.

Getting all that to happen with only a pen is quite a performance. Do children appreciate such a technical feat? I believe they do, for I believe they will marvel as I do on how the snow can be so white and lie down on the ground the way it does. How can the air be so clear and cold, and the night so still, and how did Shepard do it all with just a few scratches and specks of black ink?

From *The Horn Book Magazine*, July-August 1950.

Ernest Shepard has made his own comments on drawing Kenneth Grahame's characters and their habitats (see "Illustrating The Wind in the Willows" *earlier in this section).*

Louis Slobodkin left high school at fifteen to study drawing and sculpture at the Beaux Arts Institute of Design in New York City. For five years he drew from life for nine to twelve hours a day. During the next ten years he was an assistant sculptor. A successful sculptor himself in his thirties, he first illustrated a children's book in 1941. Three years later he received the Caldecott Medal for his illustrations for Many Moons *by James Thurber.*

PLAY WITH ME written and illustrated by Marie Hall Ets

Comment by Pamela Bianco

Play With Me is, to my mind, one of the loveliest picture books of today, both for its illustrations and for its text. The story is charming and original, and as all proper picture-book stories should, it ends in a deeply satisfying manner.

Picture books for the very young should be easy to listen to and easy to look at. In *Play With Me* Marie Hall Ets has met both these requirements completely. Without leaving anything unsaid, she has managed to write her story in as simple a manner as possible. Told in the first person, it is the story of a little girl who goes out alone into the meadow to play one morning when the sun is shining and there is dew on the grass. She sees a grasshopper sitting on the leaf of a weed. "Grasshopper, will you play with me?" the little girl asks. But when she tries to catch him he leaps away. The little girl then approaches in turn a frog, a turtle, a chipmunk, a bluejay, a rabbit and a snake. "Will you play with me?" she asks them. But none of the creatures will play with her; each in turn hurries away, startled by her noisy approach. Rejected and disconsolate, the little girl gives up and sits quietly down upon a rock beside a pond, and it is then that a wonderful thing happens. For while she is sitting there as quiet and still as can be, the creatures, no longer scared, return one by one from their hiding places to gather around her for a happy ending.

The delightful color illustrations for *Play With Me*, as simple and direct as the story itself, are drawn in black outline, and there is one picture on every page (some being double spreads), with just two lines of text beneath. The color in these drawings is delicate and harmonious. There are notes of clear yellow, flesh, white and occasionally of brown, against an oyster-gray background. In every drawing the sun is shining down upon the little girl and upon the various creatures beside her, and the clarity and freshness of morning are apparent.

It is truly difficult to draw the look and gestures of a little child, no matter how good an artist's pens or pencils may be, but in her illustrations for *Play With Me* Marie Hall Ets has succeeded . . . in doing so. The little yellow-haired girl with her white hair ribbon and her white pinafore fastened down the back by bows of tape is a very real and engaging child, alive in her every pose, movement and ges-

ture, and in her various expressions of eagerness, disappointment, sadness and joy. Throughout the entire book she moves exactly as a little girl of that age would. . . .

From *The Horn Book Magazine*, June 1956.

SUSIE THE CAT written and illustrated by Tony Palazzo

Comment by Valenti Angelo

Here is a picture book which expresses a wholeness of spirit in a fancy-free language known perhaps only to children — and to some grownups who still cherish the magic and charm of simply told stories and pictures. The illustrations are not the "sophisticated" excursions prevalent in some picture books today.

Susie the Cat written and and illustrated by Tony Palazzo is my choice . . . because of its simple and direct charm, both in the telling of the story and in the making of the pictures. I am attracted to it by a feeling of playfulness; of being in harmony with children and animals in an adventure. The pictures that adorn every page are completely coordinated with the text. They enlighten the child's vision — making it easier for the reader to grasp the ideal alliance between story and illustration. Susie the cat becomes a lovable pet, and one feels a friendly bond between the child and the animal, so well defined in simple line and shading are the drawings presented.

There is no evidence in the drawings of the artist's attempt to teach youngsters a new art idiom

Marie Hall Ets was always interested in art, although her first career was in social work. Through her work with children, she became intrigued with their drawings and and this eventually led to her creating books for children. Several of her books have been Caldecott Medal Honor Books and she won the medal itself in 1960 for Nine Days to Christmas.

Pamela Bianco's first exhibit of her drawings was in Turin when she was eleven years old; her second in London, when she was fourteen. At sixteen she came to America to live and her work was shown in New York. Entirely self-taught, her illustration for children's books has great individuality.

Tony Palazzo was an art director for several well-known magazines, had one-man shows, and exhibited in museums. He began illustrating and writing children's books in 1946.

Valenti Angelo was born in Italy and came to America as a young boy. He took evening art classes and trained himself by studying in libraries and museums. He has illustrated well over two hundred books, many of which have been in the American Institute of Graphic Arts Fifty Books of the Year exhibits.

— which in many cases is turning the art of illustrating children's books into a state of confusion, especially among school teachers, librarians and, most of all, parents. The pictures are pure. Technique, form and coloring become united. In other words, they remain pictorial statements, unfolding a story made easier to understand by virtue of its lack of mannerisms.

It is my belief that there are too many artists working today as illustrators of children's books who, fearing themselves old-fashioned, are trying to make their work appear "modern" by affecting mannerisms and eccentric innovations. . . .

The drawing clearly expresses the meaning of simplicity in delineation. Notice the feeling of anticipation in posture, movement and grace, defined with lifelike fancy. A switch of the tail, eyes gleaming and whiskers awry: "She perked up very quickly." The generous space given each picture is essential. Especially when children and animals are at play.

Excerpts from the article which appeared in *The Horn Book Magazine*, March-April 1950.

CHARLOTTE AND THE WHITE HORSE written by Ruth Krauss

Illustrated by Maurice Sendak

Comment by Barbara Cooney

I have singled out Maurice Sendak's illustrations for *Charlotte and the White Horse* as my choice . . . for Mr. Sendak, in collaboration with Ruth Krauss, has cast a spell over me with this little book. Both the words and the pictures are so simple and apparently artless that I almost hesitate to comment for fear of breaking the spell. I have been an admirer of Mr. Sendak's work ever since I first came across his jolly little children. They are very real, often very funny and always touching. Though his tenderness for little children still fills the pictures, in *Charlotte and the White Horse* Mr. Sendak has departed from his usual sunny, gay, every-day reality and has given us an other-worldly

dreamlike quality. Miss Krauss' words are linked inseparably to the misty moonlit pictures. The meaning of the words is deepened by the pictures; the feeling of the pictures is strengthened by the words. Which is as it should be. Together, they give us a lyric poem, for the eyes as well as for the ears.

It is the love story of a little girl and Milky Way, her horse. The drawing matches the story in its simplicity. The tender moonlit colors enhance the tender dreamlike quality of the words. When the threat of separation from her beloved horse fills the little girl's heart with sadness, the threat in the shape of a monumental father looms in melancholy shadows. When the gladness of never more to part arrives, as poets place their mistresses in happy landscapes filled with flowers and birds, so Mr. Sendak surrounds Charlotte and Milky Way with flowers and birds and sunshine. And Charlotte and her horse gallop through the early, misty springtime morning. And all the world is full of love. That is all. It is very simple and quite perfect.

I will make no comment on Mr. Sendak's technique, for it seems to me that he has submerged all mannerisms to the ideal point where nothing stands between what he has to say and the observer.

From *The Horn Book Magazine*, August 1956.

Maurice Sendak wrote in his biographical note in Illustrators of Children's Books: 1957-1966 *that his basic aim as an illustrator is "to let the story speak for itself, with my pictures as a kind of background music — music in the right style and always in tune with the words."*

Barbara Cooney has always been adept at fitting media and techniques to the spirit of the book she is illustrating.

CHANTICLEER AND THE FOX by Geoffrey Chaucer
Adapted and illustrated by Barbara Cooney

Comment by Aldren A. Watson

I like Barbara Cooney's *Chanticleer and the Fox* because it has succeeded in becoming a good, illustrated book. It has been well designed, in a manner appropriate to the period of the story's origin, and yet it has a subtle sense of reality. The arrangement of the house, barnyard with its woven sapling fence, trim pig house, and frugally pruned shade trees leave the reader with a strong desire to wander into the pictures. It would be good to toss the thrifty hens some corn, push an affectionate hand deep into the sheep's wool nap, or watch the pigs greedily nuzzling up every last crumb from the wooden trough. But there is nothing quaint, or contrived, or facile in the drawings. With sparing detail they have been honestly drawn to "illustrate" the simple story.

To lure, coax, or lead the reader to take part in such a story is an art; but to have combined art and artistry in such an ancient and repeatedly published tale as that of *Chanticleer* is an achievement. It has the look of having appeared now for the first time. For all its old world charm, the setting satisfies the demands of truth, and the characters take on life, although the pictures are built to a rather set pattern of the medieval tapestry,

Printed in five powerful and controlled flat colors, these pictures take their place on the pages, relate to the type matter, and are neither overpowered by the type nor steal the show.

Barbara Cooney wrote in her biographical note in Illustrators of Children's Books: 1957-1966 *that "I had always thought: once you succeed, change. So after scratchboard I tried pen and ink, pen and ink with wash, casein, collage, water color, acrylics — trying to fit the medium and techniques to the spirit of the book."*

Aldren A. Watson, who attended Yale and studied at the Art Students League in New York, is the experienced and versatile illustrator of close to two hundred books for children and adults. He has also been a cartographer for Time *magazine, a teacher of hand bookbinding, and the designer of a type face called Watson-Cameron.*

The book (and therefore some of the pictures) suffers from the common ailment of side sewing, a disease for which modern book medicine has found no cure. Although the book arts have made advances — and some very dramatic ones, too — while one cure has been discovered, still another has been overlooked. A quick reference to some of of the block books made approximately at the same time that Chaucer was writing, will show that old sewing was better than new — and that many of the old books are still in one piece. Not only that, but they will swing open and lie flat! If we need to sew books on tapes, or use a heavier gauge of thread, then it may be up to the machine designers. To anyone who has done much hand bookbinding, it appears probable that the increase in number of folios in each signature would materially improve the strength of book sewing. *Chanticleer* is as impressive an example as any of the propensity our books have of clanging shut when the holder relaxes his vigilance for even an instant. This feature is most clearly demonstrated when the reader is also holding a child on his lap. If the topic seems out of place here, I would make it pertinent by adding that this is a handsome book: it would have been that much more attractive if it had not been riveted so solidly from the side.

From *The Horn Book Magazine*, October 1960.

TWO LITTLE TRAINS written by Margaret Wise Brown
Illustrated by Jean Charlot

Comment by Maurice Sendak

Not long ago as I was sorting through a pile of books that had belonged to me as a child, I picked up one of my favorites and something almost magical occurred — by simply holding the book in my hands I was able to relive the delicious first experience of reading it. The musty, yellow smell of the pages brought back the summertime and the lazy days when I sat on the hot stone steps in front of my house, absorbed in the lives of the Prince and the Pauper — the streets quiet except for the sing-song of the old-clothes man making his way from backyard to backyard: "Buy old clothes! Buy old clothes!" *The Prince and the Pauper* and the sing-song of the old-clothes man are forever one in my memory. And the illustrations in the book are so much a part of the story that I can't remember one without the other.

The book was a miracle to me when I was a child. Now, as an adult and a children's book illustrator, I realize how hard it is to bring about one of these "miracles" in bookmaking. Now I know that it was a combination of things that made *The Prince and the Pauper* such an intense experience; the story, the size of the type, the illustrations, the weight and shape of the book, the binding, the shiny colored picture on the cover, the very smell of the pages.

A more recent book that, for me, has achieved this miracle is Margaret Wise Brown's *Two Little Trains*. The story is a little masterpiece of subtle understatement. Jean Charlot is completely in tune with the story. His pictures do not merely enhance the looks of the book. They live with the words in perfect harmony. They go off into wonderful elaborations and amplifications of the text. His choice of colors is a breathing into life of the very color of Miss Brown's words. The poignancy and drama of the journey to the West are felt by Charlot, as in:

> Look down, look down
> Below the bridge,
> At the deep dark river
> Going West,

where his picture of the black waters is filled with an eerie sequence of fishes all devouring each other.

The story reveals so much more than it actually says. It is a perilous journey to the West, with rain and snow and dust storm. The two little trains chug-a-chug their way up the steep mountains that come beyond the plain, and a Charlot mountain goat arches its back in terror at sight of them.

What I love most is the humor with which Charlot draws his sturdy little children completely undaunted by the severities of the trip. It rains and out come the umbrellas and wrap-around blankets. No fear is written on the children's faces. They sleep in undisturbed innocence under the fat half moon while the trains hurry on. On reaching the edge of the West, the children promptly climb out of their clothes and jump into the ocean that is big and that is blue.

I relish, too, the bobbing heads of the cattle and geese aboard the two little trains. Here again the simplicity of drawing is a perfect reflection of the meaningful simplicity of the story. The marvelous black-and-white snow scene, with the cattle ducking their heads down so that only their horns show and the passive geese with snow dripping from their bills, is perhaps my favorite. Yet, really, I have no favorite in the whole book. No picture could be lifted out of its text; they are made for each other.

The strong square look of the book is just right, and the firm, black type couldn't be better. There is nothing "prissy" about this book. How easy it would have been to misunderstand completely Miss Brown's real intentions and to make it a "cute" book! It is a rugged saga of our expanding country on one level and, for me, a very personal experience on the other. I heartily recommend it to anyone interested in the little "miracles" of bookmaking.

From *The Horn Book Magazine*, August 1955.

Jean Charlot, an American citizen born in France, went to Mexico in his twenties and began his career as an artist there. He has been a mural painter, an easel painter, a teacher, has done archeological research, perfected a new process of lithographic printing, and illustrated children's books.

Maurice Sendak, who attended the Art Students League in New York, felt that there was never any question as to his eventual profession — writer and illustrator of children's books. In 1964 he was awarded the Caldecott Medal for Where the Wild Things Are.

A BELL FOR URSLI written by Selina Chönz

Illustrated by Alois Carigiet

Comment by Marc Simont

The final judgment upon looking at a picture book — as in looking at a painting, piece of sculpture, reading a book, etc. — rests on the amount of enjoyment we derive from it. When methods and techniques become so important they can't be overlooked, the intensity of enjoyment value is cut.

When I was asked to mention a recent picture book that I liked, *A Bell for Ursli* came to my mind, but, in order to give specific reasons for my choice, I had to go back and take another look.

The illustrations by Alois Carigiet have three important points in their favor — first, they are in harmony with the text; second, they are beautiful pictures; third, they hold together as a unit.

As illustrations they complement the story perfectly. Color is used for what it can do to a picture, not just as a means to define objects. When an object can be used to advantage, however, as in the case of the great, big beautiful bell, the opportunity is not overlooked. Aside from working well with the story, the illustrations hold their own as individual pictures, and this is done without disturbing the cohesiveness of the book.

It is a well-planned, beautifully executed piece of work done in excellent taste.

From *The Horn Book Magazine*, March-April 1951.

Alois Carigiet, a Swiss artist, served as an apprentice in a painting shop, and after painting many posters and creating theatrical scenery as a commercial artist, he made a name for himself as a mural painter. In 1966 his illustrations for children's books brought him the first Hans Christian Andersen Medal given to an illustrator — the medal being presented biennially by the International Board on Books for Young People for the body of an artist's work.

Marc Simont grew up in France, Spain, and the United States and studied at art schools in Paris. He received the Caldecott Medal in 1957 for his illustrations for A Tree Is Nice *by Janice May Udry.*

THE SNOWSTORM written by Selina Chönz

Illustrated by Alois Carigiet

Comment by Kurt Werth

The Snowstorm . . . is one of my favorite books. . . . The text in the English translation is a simplified version of the original German story and easy to read even for young children. The pictures are beautifully reproduced and the book as a whole has atmosphere, charm and lightness. Alois Carigiet has departed from the heavy outlines of his first book, *A Bell for Ursli.* His drawings now are softer in line and color and children will feel a relationship with their own art work.

Snow is always a fascinating experience for the young. I remember my first drawings as a child were often inspired by the merry happenings of a winter day. Snowball fights and ice skating on a frozen pond, trudging home dead tired and hungry as wolves after hour-long activities on the ice, thick snowflakes coming down — this was winter. These scenes I tried to put down again and again on the loose pages of my sketchbook.

I find this spirit again in Carigiet's pictures — they are felt and done with the heart of a child. All the details which are so important, epic and humorous, the accuracy of the scene, the nearness of nature expressed very realistically, are designed in a great style.

One of my favorite illustrations, the scene in the barn where Ursli is feeding a calf, with the horse, the cows, goats, and sheep at their mangers, is an example of powerful drawing and harmonious colors. The grain of the boards, horizontal and vertical, the texture, the movement of the lines, and the naïve, refined forms are a great achievement. I like especially how the warmth of a stable is depicted, with the oil lamp shedding its light on the scene, contrasted by the wintry cold outside shown by a few snowflakes in the open door. The vivid colors in the drawing of the children's party at the

Kurt Werth studied at the Academy for Graphic Arts in Leipzig and began his career in his native Germany. When he was not allowed to work during Hitler's regime, he fled to the United States with his family. Eventually he found work in the children's book field, and has illustrated the stories of many different authors.

end of the book, with music, dancing and eating, should arouse the delight of every child. It is the gayest picture and at the same time the effective finale of the story.

From *The Horn Book Magazine*, February 1960.

TIM TO THE RESCUE written and illustrated by Edward Ardizzone

Comment by Helen Stone

If without corrosive reservations one welcomes Edward Ardizzone's *Tim to the Rescue* so happily, there must be good reasons why, and faint praise is not in order. From a spirited jacket through page after page are drawings in pen, free and vigorous, almost of Daumier bravura, well-suited to a theme, the excitement of which is conveyed in fast moving vivid *line*, and organized, not contrived for too obvious design, into rhythmic *compositions*, like well-conceived choreography. This is an effective foil for an earnest little boy of most delicate manliness. Tim versus the weather, posed birdlike in the rigging on his dancer's feet, is sketched with the utmost knowledge of little boys, as again with Ginger, in a puddle before a quite comic opera, but perfectly seaworthy, captain. All illustrations are

Edward Ardizzone drew as a schoolboy in England, but before he could take up art as a career he had to spend seven years as an office worker. At thirty-five he wrote and illustrated the first Little Tim *book for his children. Publication soon followed, as did a career in children's book illustration interrupted only by World War II. He was the first to win England's Kate Greenaway Medal, established and given annually by the Library Association to a British artist, for distinguished work in the field of illustration of children's books.*

Helen Stone studied at New York School of Fine and Applied Art, the Art Students League and in Paris. For many years she was mainly interested in painting, until, in her forties she began illustrating children's books. Even though she used many different techniques for a variety of stories she usually did her own separations. Her comments on Ardizzone relate to her experience as a painter as well as an illustrator.

unrestricted and compelling; mood dominates manner, and all is wit.

Form is indicated fluently in mellow line or crisp, as needed, with quick perception, and a well-rounded artist's personality is clear in composition relationships, fidelity to types and situations, not to mention excellent drawing.

Masses here are stated admirably in values, with rapid diagonal slashes and daring cross hatch. In such fulsome expression is seen no cautious niggling about for surface effects so often confused with art, affectations of any kind being blessedly missing from the work of Mr. Ardizzone.

As to depicting *types*, this artist tosses them off in a gust of sounds, tastes and smells. Their sea dog speech caught in waggish balloons, but not too often; their secret vanities (see Third Mate's cabin) ; the grousing and heady mixtures (in mess and galley) ; Tim the Scribe (see letters home) ; their common weakness, the common cat (seen everywhere) — all are keenly observed. And where, oh where, is a sight so hilarious as Ginger, the barber's Nemesis, transfixed under his bramble of hair, except in some of the good examples of genre illustration of the eighteenth and nineteenth centuries, including Cruikshank?

Color, where used, floats in transparent washes of blues, stormy greens and sturdy siennas to umber. Reds have a song. Love's labor is saved for our enjoyment in beautiful reproductions, and informal hand lettering carries the charming and reticent text.

Finally the key to all is an *attitude*. Along with the fun a sweet seriousness toward children could hardly be better shown than in drawings of sea longing (p. 1) , attention to lessons, a proud home-coming, and above all in Mr. Ardizzone's conception of Tim himself. The story, the pictures, everything, reflect and bear his hero out. He is very small in such great seas, but he sparkles beautifully, and can be seen at any distance. Long life to little Tim!

From *The Horn Book Magazine*, May-June 1950.

A rabbit was sitting behind the oak tree.
He was wiggling his nose and nibbling a flower.

16

"Rabbit," I said, "will you play with me?"
And I tried to catch him, but he ran to the woods.

17

46. Illustration by Marie Hall Ets for *Play With Me* written and illustrated by Marie Hall Ets, Viking, 1955, 7½ x 10.

47. Illustration by Tony Palazzo for *Susie the Cat* written and illustrated by Tony Palazzo, Viking, 1949, 7¾ x 10¾.

Susie's sleep was disturbed.

"This is the song of Charlotte
and Milky Way, her horse.
He was born in a stable.

48. Illustration by Maurice Sendak for *Charlotte and the White Horse* by Ruth Krauss, Harper, 1955, 6⅜ x 5⅛.

49. Illustration by Barbara Cooney for *Chanticleer and the Fox* by Geoffrey Chaucer, Crowell, 1958, 7⅜ x 10.

She had only three large sows, three cows, and also a sheep called Molly.

A FOR THE ARK written and illustrated by Roger Duvoisin

Comment by Nora S. Unwin

For many years I have been an ardent admirer of the work of Roger Duvoisin. Realizing that I could write happily about any one of a great number of books adorned by his distinguished hand, I chose one in particular. The battered and coverless picture book that lies in my lap at the moment is *A for the Ark*. Its dilapidated condition is eloquent proof that it has been the loved choice of countless small readers and embryo artists long before I seized upon it. And this gives me added pleasure in choosing to write of it now.

Perhaps a long-founded admiration for good lettering has somewhat influenced my choice. I must admit that the beautiful basic shapeliness and balance of these Roman capitals gives me deep satisfaction. When coupled with Roger Duvoisin's lively, sensitive and masterly draughtsmanship, there is a treat for the eye on every page!

Every other double spread of this picture alphabet is in full color, the lower half of each page being devoted to a continuous sort of picture-frieze while the upper part carries the bold, simple text and elegant capitals in alternative shades of blue and coral red. The entire treatment is deceptively simple, with Roger Duvoisin's inimitable vitality and freedom of line. Each double spread has a satisfying sense of balance and design that never interferes with the legibility of the text but carries the

eye on comfortably, along with the gradually accumulating alphabet, and readily invites the turning of the page.

With the utmost economy of means, either in color, tone, or line, Duvoisin portrays a mood and gives marvelous characterization of each animal called into the Ark. With an apparent flick of his pen he shows us the supercilious stateliness of the llamas, the eager inquisitiveness of the foxes and the slinkiness of the leopards. We can literally hear the thundering of the horses' hooves, the clatter of goat feet, and feel the beautiful rhythmic jump of the kangaroos. And then there are the sly touches of humor; the flowers in Mrs. Kangaroo's pocket, the swaying angle of the polite black bears, the little leaping frogs, that sideways glance of the wolf at the ferret, and the whole company depicted again on the end papers.

The drama of the Noah's Ark story moves consistently and progressively with the gathering clouds growing bigger and blacker on every page. In the color pages, the deepening ominous tones are intensified by the glorious red touch, now large, now small, that is Noah's robe.

There seems to be just the right amount of detail in the pictures, plus a certain amount of informative natural history, for a young child. But there is never a sense of overcrowding. The wide blank spaces are carefully planned and play their part. The vitality and humor of the line drawings beside the colorful lettered squares at the end are a feast for the eye, whatever the age of the viewer. . . .

From *The Horn Book Magazine*, April 1959.

Roger Duvoisin, born in Switzerland, was brought up in an artistic household, where drawing and painting came to him naturally. He later studied at Ecole des Arts Decoratifs in Paris, designed scenery, painted murals and posters, and worked in ceramics and textiles. He came to America as art director of a textile firm. A book drawn for his son was published, and led to his illustrating many more, some of which he also wrote. In 1948 he received the Caldecott Medal for his illustrations for White Snow, Bright Snow *by Alvin Tresselt.*

Nora S. Unwin came to the United States from her native England after the second World War. Her paintings and wood engravings and prints have been widely exhibited. She has illustrated, and written, a number of books for children.

THE THANKSGIVING STORY written by Alice Dalgliesh

Illustrated by Helen Sewell

Comment by Garry MacKenzie

It sometimes seems to me that people who look at children's books, and occasionally talk about them, have a static conception of both the author and the illustrator. They seem to forget that a book represents a moment of development in a continuous artistic history that stretches both before and after — or, rather, *two* moments: one for the writer and one for the illustrator. Of course, many artists go on repeating themselves, but the good ones don't.

I say people tend to forget this when they talk about children's books in a way they don't forget it when they talk about the periods of Picasso or the phases of Henry James. But one of the beautiful things about a good illustrator's work is the way it changes over a number of books. Of course, the changes should never represent a complete break. They should emphasize what is centrally significant in the artist by underlining what is continuous in his development — what *doesn't* change.

I know few contemporary illustrators whose work shows such remarkable evidence at one and the same time of continuity and change as that of Helen Sewell. Since her earlier books, say, *A First Bible* or *A Round of Carols*, both of which appeared in the 'thirties, down to *The Thanksgiving Story*, or *Grimm's Tales* which she illustrated in collaboration with Madeleine Gekiere in 1954, there has been a continuous movement, but in directions that were indicated from the first. For example, take the illustration for "I Saw Three Ships" in *A Round of Carols*. The picture of the three miniature ships afloat on a highly stylized ocean clearly shows the influence of medieval illustration, but somewhat softened and sweetened. In her illustration for Grimm, the medieval influence has been strengthened and made the vehicle of a more rigorously personal vision. Much of the earlier sentiment is absent, but is replaced by a formal structural iconography that is heraldic in conception. I should like to mention the illustrations for this edition as the most successful example of collaboration between artists that I know of. The almost menacing quality of Miss Sewell's drawings in this book embodies that element of the sinister which is one half of the folk world given us by Grimm. The other half, of fantasy and dream, is incorporated in the lacy, free lines of Miss Gekiere. Together they make a perfect whole.

The flexibility and range of Miss Sewell's talent are suggested by her pictures for *The Thanksgiving Story* which appeared in the same year as *Grimm's Tales*. In this book, the brooding atmosphere that permeated the Grimm pictures, and which was suggestive of medieval woodcuts, is chastened to an air of early American sobriety. The suggestion of the woodcut is still present in the flat patterning of the over-all design in each picture in *The Thanksgiving Story*, but the emotional note is no longer portentous. Gone are the sombre figures with their air of veiled menace. Grimm's murky world of submerged terrors is replaced by the crisp angularity of the Puritans — the old European shadows by the cool light and air of early New England. One of the extraordinary things about this book is the sureness and tact with which Miss Sewell evokes the cyclic progression of the seasons in this austere Puritan world — from the decorous, disciplined spring to the relentless judgment of winter. That an artist should be able, in consecutive books, to catch the tone of two such different imaginative worlds is a very fine achievement.

From *The Horn Book Magazine*, October 1956.

Helen Sewell illustrated a number of adult books for The Limited Editions Club, as well as over sixty children's books.

Garry MacKenzie has lived and studied both in England and the United States. His own work, which began with his appreciation of classical illustration and Chinese and Japanese painting, has also taken into consideration more abstract elements.

CROW BOY written and illustrated by Taro Yashima

Comment by Nicolas Mordvinoff

A great many picture books are published each year. Among them are some good ones, but only a few that are excellent. One of the most striking published recently is *Crow Boy* by Taro Yashima. It does not belong in a class with painstakingly realistic representation or with sweet stereotyped stylizations. Neither could it be placed among the tasteful sophistications of the currently fashionable styles. It is therefore not altogether surprising that it did not attract more considerable attention.

The snow came down
And covered the ground,
And the two little trains going West.

And they got white and furry,
And still in a hurry
They puffed and chugged to the West.

50. Illustration by Jean Charlot for *Two Little Trains* by Margaret Wise Brown, Scott, 1949, 7¾ x 9½.

51. Illustration by Edward Ardizzone for *Tim to the Rescue* written and illustrated by Edward Ardizzone, Oxford, 1949, 7½ x 10.

Tim only went on deck to rescue his companion Ginger. It was a very gallant action and I am going to ask the Royal

Humane Society to give him a gold medal." -Cheers from the crew-"Alaska Pete and Old Joe", the Captain continued, "were very brave

52. Illustration by Alois Carigiet for *A Bell for Ursli* by Selina Chönz, Oxford, 1950, 12⅛ x 9½.

The design is unusual. This large book seems even bigger than it is, yet not big enough for the colorful compositions that make the space surrounding them gleam magically more white than white. The sweeping rhythm of the picture carries one through endless surprises; a page with one simple design will be followed by another filled with four or five small but well-composed pictures, sometimes suggesting no more than "a patch of cloth on a boy's shoulder," the wooden top of a desk with a knife or a pencil, streaks of rain on a window. The bold expressionism with a touch of humor, tempered by an oriental delicacy, blends in a rare poetic mood and carries through from the first to the last page — not to ignore the end papers, which are among the most beautiful designs.

Those who know the intricacies of the color separation technique for direct contact offset reproduction will be surprised by the ease with which Taro Yashima has mastered the medium. It is interesting to see the progress achieved since one of his earlier attempts in *The Village Tree*. Now the results are worthy of the best lithographers. With no more than the three basic colors, not counting the black, he fills his pictures with all the colors of the prism, combining the bright light of the Impressionists with a refined elegance reminiscent of Japanese paintings. The exuberance of his imagination held within the restraining limits of the technique is the mark of a draughtsman expressing himself with freedom and spontaneity and of an artist with a quality I praise above all — sincerity.

Since this has been an artist's choice, I have limited myself to the art work which, in a picture book, can by no means be considered independently, the essential quality being the unity of illustration, text, and design. In this case we have a complete homogeneity, and if each picture can be enjoyed separately, so can the poetry of this simple story in lines such as these:

"He showed how crows cry early in the morning.

"He showed how crows cry when the village people have some unhappy accident.
"He showed how crows call when they are happy and gay."

From *The Horn Book Magazine*, December 1956.

THE TWO REDS written by Will Illustrated by Nicolas
Comment by Fritz Eichenberg

Tradition can be a good thing if we use it to give greater strength, more skill and beauty to our contemporary creative expression. Tradition can also be an easy chair into which we settle back comfortably and stubbornly, sit on our *status quo* and refuse to be budged.

It takes courage to innovate. You have to leave the easy chair if you want to blaze a new trail, and there is no telling what dangers you are going to face. In the children's book field it may mean facing angry librarians, bad reviews and indifferent salesmen. . . .

It takes . . . great courage to employ an artist who is new in the children's book field and obviously belongs to the modern school and then not to tamper with him nor cramp his style.

The editor realizes . . . that one of the greatest contributions an illustrator can make to the success of a book is his untrammeled enthusiasm — freedom to create, according to his God-given talent. . . .

The Two Reds shows the hard work only to the initiated. It still looks casual, fresh, "contempor-

Taro Yashima grew up in Japan and attended the Imperial Art Academy of Tokyo. Later he came to America and studied at the Art Students League in New York. He has had one-man shows and his paintings are in several major museums. He began illustrating and writing children's books for his daughter, Momo.

Both Fritz Eichenberg and Nicolas (the pseudonym of Nicolas Mordvinoff) are winners of the Caldecott Medal.

Nicolas Mordvinoff, born in Russia, escaped with his parents during the Russian Revolution. He studied Latin, Philosophy and Languages at the University of Paris and painted as a student of Leger. He illustrated children's books, came to the United States, and won the 1952 Caldecott Medal for Finders Keepers.

70

ary.'' The days and weeks of filing down the manuscript to a clean and sparkling economy of words, in close cooperation with artist and editor; the weeks and months of working and reworking the illustrations and still having them look spontaneous; the hard job of separating the colors without losing the fresh feeling of the original; the careful matching of artist's paint and printer's ink; and a production department with unending patience, skill and understanding for a job well done — all these combine to make *The Two Reds* a book that artists and children instinctively like, and also those adults who are at heart artists or children! . . .

From *The Horn Book Magazine*, July-August 1951.

MY FRIEND MAC written by May McNeer

Illustrated by Lynd Ward

Comment by Laura Bannon

Overwhelmed by the different kinds of attractive picture books on the market, I narrowed my choice to the recent books that contribute an original story to children's literature. I selected *My Friend Mac.*

This is the story of a lonely Canadian boy who finds a new friend, a baby moose. Without being literal, Lynd Ward has filled the illustrations with all the realism and human appeal of the text. And he has added something to the spirit and imagination of the story.

Lynd Ward might well be called the dean of American children's books illustrators. He is represented in this volume by articles in Section I, Section III, and Section IV.

Laura Bannon was both teacher and artist, studying at a state teachers' college in Michigan and at the School of the Art Institute of Chicago. Her extensive work as a painter and her pioneer work in progressive art education in the Junior Department of the Chicago Art Institute led to a book for adults, Mind Your Child's Art, *and to her writing and illustrating books for children.*

A flat muted tone works hand in hand with the black drawings to give space and depth to the North Woods. A few tall trees become a deep forest. A skillful use of empty spaces helps to spell out the loneliness of the small still boy. Through Lynd Ward's masterly control of perspective and knowledge of structure, the moose grows in massiveness from a calf to full maturity without crowding the margins. And as any artist knows, this is no easy trick, especially when the small boy, who must be large enough to carry his part in the drama, ends by sharing the page with an obstreperous friend who has grown until his head is as large as the boy.

No matter how excellent are the parts of a picture book — the story, the picture spots, the layout of type block with illustration, all the details of format — it can't be a work of art unless these parts are related closely enough to enjoy each other's company. And yet, during the process of production there are many chances for any one of these parts to become altered enough to quarrel with its companions.

If all the different professional groups that work to produce one little picture book were counted on the fingers of two hands, there wouldn't be enough fingers. And, to some extent, these separate groups have no communication with each other. A platemaker may allow a change in color without knowing the artist had a special reason for using that particular hue. A change in the color of the jacket or covercloth can destroy the color unity of the book. A different binding can disrupt marginal spaces. Dozens of small, unintentional changes may creep in.

And so it is a distinct pleasure to laud a picture book that has so gracefully survived its production, all of a piece, as has *My Friend Mac.*

From *The Horn Book Magazine*, April 1961.

They walked along the shore and there seemed to be nothing but sand and sand and more sand. They cut some sweet-smelling branches of juniper, a kind of evergreen, and took them back to the ship. That night the settlers had a warm wood fire.

Some of the women and children on the *Mayflower* went ashore as soon as they could and had a wash day. There was a pond of fresh water near the beach. It was good to have clean, fresh clothes again.

53. Illustration by Helen Sewell for *The Thanksgiving Story* by Alice Dalgliesh, Scribner, 1954, 8 x 10.

54. Illustration by Nicolas Mordvinoff for *The Two Reds* by William Lipkind, Harcourt, 1950, 8⅜ x 10¾.

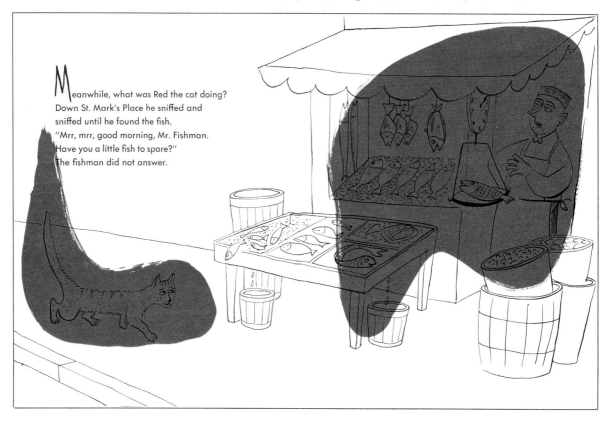

Meanwhile, what was Red the cat doing? Down St. Mark's Place he sniffed and sniffed until he found the fish.
"Mrr, mrr, good morning, Mr. Fishman. Have you a little fish to spare?"
The fishman did not answer.

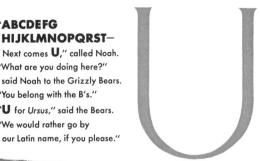

**"ABCDEFGHIJKLMNOP
QRS—T**'s next," called Noah.
"**T** for Tigers;
T for Toads;
T for Titmice;
T for the Turkeys;
T for the Turtles.
Tiger could swallow all the T's,
but let's not worry.
Everyone will be safe on my Ark."

**"ABCDEFG
HIJKLMNOPQRST—**
Next comes **U**," called Noah.
"What are you doing here?"
said Noah to the Grizzly Bears.
"You belong with the B's."
"**U** for *Ursus*," said the Bears.
"We would rather go by
our Latin name, if you please."

55. Illustration by Roger Duvoisin for *A for the Ark* written and illustrated by Roger Duvoisin, Lothrop, 1952, 8¼ x 10⅜.

56. Illustration by Taro Yashima for *Crow Boy* written and illustrated by Taro Yashima, Viking, 1958, 8⅞ x 12.

Then Mr. Isobe explained how Chibi had learned those calls — leaving his home for school at dawn,

and arriving home at sunset,

every day for six long years.

Every one of us cried, thinking how much we had been wrong to Chibi all those long years.

A PAIR OF RED CLOGS written by Masako Matsuno

Illustrated by Kazue Mizumura

Comment by Leonard Everett Fisher

An artist called upon to exercise his judgment in selecting the work of another which he finds irresistible is sometimes confronted by an academic dilemma. The esthetic rules by which he governs his whole artistic being are not always compatible with the selections of his unpredictable subjective inclinations. Challenges to his artistic ideas do occur. Those that are attractive to him should never be denied the pleasure of his exploration.

In choosing *A Pair of Red Clogs* . . . I was influenced by a fascinating combination of ingredients. Here is a book written by a Japanese author exhibiting the essence of sensitivity and delicateness that we often associate with the Far East. Here too are illustrations by a Japanese artist capturing every tone created by the author and by a venerable culture. All this is aimed at a young audience whose traditions are vastly different.

I am relieved that the book was not illustrated by a Westerner, enamored of Oriental art, who understands far less of the Oriental mood than he supposes. Miss Mizumura communicates the author's intent with great clarity while bringing the consciousness of her own heritage into sharp focus. Her use of Western pictorial devices such as schematic lighting situations (i.e., using natural or artificial light to arbitrarily produce graphic effects contrary to the optical laws determined by that light source) effectively bridges the diverse styles of East and West. These devices never succeed in displacing the over-all-high-keyed, flat tone and line image of Oriental artistic refinement.

Although her color contributes to this total effect, there are areas that show Miss Mizumura to be somewhat less than a master of acetate color separation.* There are also bits of scratchy rendering that are unnecessary. Nevertheless, in the control of a modulating black line to give shape and personality to an object Miss Mizumura is superb. That line, which moves so confidently wherever one looks, capricious here, sober there, is the basis of the wonderful animation in her characters and arrangements.

The format of this book never disturbs Miss Mizumura's gifted hand. The first and last impression is made by the content itself, rather than by an overawing presentation of that content. The inseparable ideas of this author and artist are allowed to be the prime reason for the book's existence. Altogether it is a visually delightful literary experience.

From *The Horn Book Magazine*, October 1961.
* *Editor's Note: In 1975, some fifteen years after the above book was published, Kazue Mizumura was a featured speaker at the first International Children's Book Festival held at the Boston Public Library. Her books and her talk both proved her to have mastered the difficult art of making separations of great subtlety.*

Kazue Mizumura studied at the Women's Art Institute in Tokyo and after coming to the United States in 1955 for further study at Pratt Institute, she became a textile designer. In 1959 she was asked to illustrate The Cheerful Heart *and commissions to illustrate other books with Japanese background followed. Eventually she was able to break away from illustrating only Oriental material, but all her work shows an interesting dualism.*

Leonard Everett Fisher received a B.F.A. and M.F.A. from Yale School of Fine Arts; has traveled on a Pulitzer Art Fellowship; and has been dean of an art school. He has successfully managed a full double career as painter and muralist, illustrator and writer.

NIBBLE NIBBLE written by Margaret Wise Brown

Illustrated by Leonard Weisgard

Comment by Richard Floethe

One of the most charming books for children I have seen in recent years is *Nibble Nibble*. . . . The two words serene, tranquil, come to mind when one is searching for words to describe this imaginative book illustrated throughout in two tones of green and black. True, there is a certain sameness resulting from this limitation of color, but the cleverness with which Mr. Weisgard exploits his limitation fills me with admiration. Every illustrator dreams of the books he would like to do using a full range of color. For reasons of expense publishers rarely can afford to allow an artist this lux-

ury. He is told arbitrarily how many colors he can
can use (in this case, green halftone and black line
cut), and out of this combination he must create
what magic he can.

And magic is precisely what Mr. Weisgard
creates. When we go with him "Deep In The
Green Stemmed World" the wonderfully cool,
damp lushness of wild growing things pervades our
senses. One can almost smell the odor of summer
and hear the buzz of his bumble bee. In the section
entitled "In the Darkness Of The Sea" there are
pert little fish grinning at us from their watery
depth and a giant whale flipping his tail in such a
way that one quite expects to be covered with salt
spray. And when Mr. Weisgard comes to the selection of poems about animals he has still other
moods in store for us. Leaping bunnies, a ridicu-
lous bear being worsted by a butterfly, feathery
grasses, landscapes of depth and charm, they are
all there, bringing Miss Brown's gentle, childlike
verses into more vivid perspective. Only in two
illustrations do humans intrude — and I use the
word intrude advisedly, for although they are
treated with considerable humor by the artist, they
might better have been left out of this collection in
which the animals and beautiful growing things
come to us with such a bright and natural charm
that one is a trifle jarred at the presentation of
humans crying over a sliced onion.

My admiration does not stop at Mr. Weisgard's
individual illustrations; it is probably the artist's
concept of the book as a whole that I admire most.
Everything has been considered with infinite taste.
The placement of the illustrations in relation to
each page and length of text gives a satisfying
sense of balance throughout. Nothing hit or miss
spoils the continuity of mood. From the lovely
jacket and title page we are led in successive steps
into the world which the author had in mind to
create. For Mr. Weisgard has never forgotten that
he is the interpreter of the author's poems. He has
never sought to dominate, to shock or grasp for
attention. It is this that gives the wonderful seren-
ity to the book. The illustrations flow as simply and
as naturally as the poems. Mr. Weisgard has succeeded in bringing us a breath of true loveliness.
Nibble Nibble is a book to cherish.

From *The Horn Book Magazine*, April 1962.

THE SECRET HIDING PLACE written and illustrated by Rainey Bennett

Comment by Adrienne Adams

. . . Making a book that possesses both style and
"heart" is no simple thing. That is rare in all fields.
In the area of book illustration particularly I think
the instigators (I'm trying to avoid the word
"creators") *care* more — and it's the caring that
counts, and shows.

A large number of very good artists are turning
to books. Scratch almost any artist and you will uncover a desire to do a book. Most of us have
worked in advertising, or textiles, or display where
our work was used with advertising copy over it,
or aimed at illustrating a commercial product. A
book, however, is something you can hold in your
hand, a pure thing of your own. Between hard
covers. It can be satisfying. . . .

*Leonard Weisgard has illustrated many children's books
in a variety of media. His preference is to write, illustrate,
and design the entire book, but he is sensitive to the needs
of other writers' work. In 1947 he won the Caldecott
Medal for his illustrations for* The Little Island *by Golden
MacDonald (pseudonym of Margaret Wise Brown).*

*Richard Floethe, after his study in Germany, specialized
in graphic arts. He emigrated to America and eventually
became a teacher at the Ringling School of Art in Sara-
sota, Florida. He has illustrated many books, some of
which have been in the American Institute of Graphic
Arts Fifty Books of the Year shows.*

*Rainey Bennett grew up near Chicago and attended sev-
eral art schools there and in New York. He began his
career as a muralist and watercolorist; his paintings hang
in major museums. His art work for a large department
store's Christmas advertising led to his illustration of
books for children.*

*Adrienne Adams taught in rural Oklahoma until she
could afford three months at the American School of Design in New York. She then found free-lance work in
designing textiles and displays, painting murals, and illustrating books. Her article on "Color Separation" appears
in Section III of this book.*

57. Illustration by Lynd Ward for *My Friend Mac* by May McNeer, Houghton Mifflin, 1960, 6⅞ x 9¼.

58. Illustration by Kazue Mizamura for *A Pair of Red Clogs* by Masako Matsuno, World, 1960, 9¼ x 8.

59. Illustration by Leonard Weisgard for *Nibble Nibble* by Margaret Wise Brown, Scott, 1959, 8¼ x 10¾.

60. Illustration by Rainey Bennett for *The Secret Hiding Place* written and illustrated by Rainey Bennett, World, 1960, 10¼ x 8½.

But Little Hippo didn't want to be protected. He wanted to go exploring by himself. What fun is a walk with nineteen hippos?

. . . Currently, I'm enchanted with Rainey Bennett's *The Secret Hiding Place.* I can't say it is the illustrating alone that wins me, for it is impossible to separate the pictures from the story here. They are one unit; and, of course, they were done by one person.

This is not to say that it is an advantage when the author and artist are one. At *times* it may be, but very often the artist and writer complement one another exceedingly well, making a double richness in the completed work that a single personality and talent might not have achieved.

Here I was won by the over-all idea, full of warmth and humor, plus a leading character I could love in situations and feelings I could recognize as true for me, too.

Mr. Bennett is very clever about using reproductive problems instead of letting them use him. One of the difficulties of color reproduction is the necessity for exactness of registration of one color over another. Tightly done illustrations which call for hairline exactness of registration are particularly difficult for the artists, most of whom make their own separations. For better printing, a four-color picture must be done in black instead of the actual colors and must be redone in four layers — one for red, one for blue, one for yellow, as well as the key, or black, drawing. By using color loosely and freely, Mr. Bennett conquered this problem with ease. I wouldn't like to see color used this way in every book; I'd tire of it. But in this one I find it refreshing.

Even in the best of books there are failure spots. Returning to a book I've responded to with delight, I realize that there are uninteresting pages. Although we all strive to give equal value and strength to all our drawings, sometimes three or four especially successful pages are carrying the whole book.

In Bennett's book, however, there is remarkable evenness. I enjoy it.

From *The Horn Book Magazine,* October 1962.

III

Notes About Illustration
and Techniques

The Book Artist: Ideas and Techniques

by Lynd Ward

... It is the book for younger children whose recent growth has been most dramatically intertwined with improvements in offset printing. ...

The primary point in this dependency is economic. ... But beyond that, there are factors of importance to the book artist. The first ... is the factor of technical variety. Pen line, brush drawing, wash drawing, transparent water color, casein or gouache, crayon work, pastel, or solidly painted oil are all available to the artist and all transferable by the magic of offset to a book page. It is true that letterpress reproduction can undertake the photographic reproduction of work in all of these media, and does so regularly for the pages of our contemporary magazines. But the great aesthetic problem is that letterpress can print a drawing whose tonal qualities require translation into the dots of a halftone screen only on the coated papers that give the name "slicks" to the magazines so printed.

Such papers can and have been used for book printing, but, by common agreement, they produce a cold and unfriendly book page and have been almost universally supplanted by the offset papers.

61. Water color illustration by Uri Shulevitz for *Dawn,* words and pictures by Uri Shulevitz, Farrar, 1974, 10 x 9.

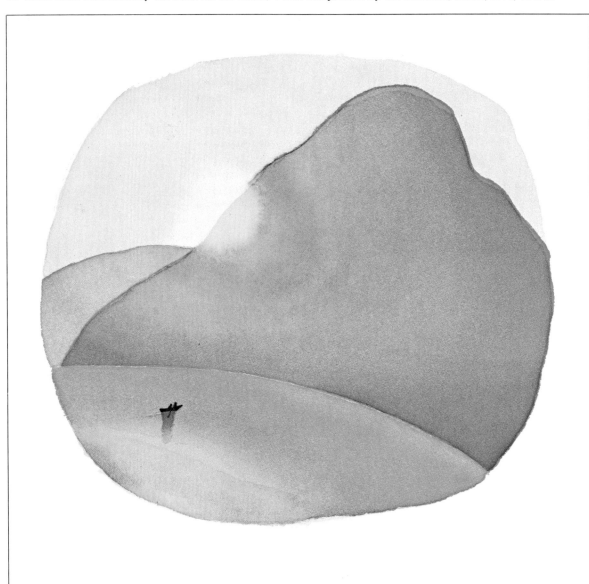

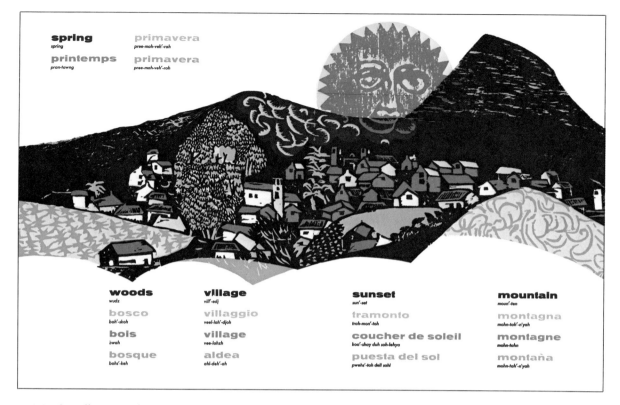

62. Woodcut illustration by Antonio Frasconi for *See Again, Say Again,* Harcourt, 1964, 10⅜ x 8¾.

The quality of these is such that they not only approximate in appearance and feel the paper that both tradition and sensibility agree is "right" for books, but they provide a background for the artist's work that is close to the drawing paper on which the original work was executed. A good offset reproduction of a delicate brush drawing will be closer to the true qualities of the artist's original than a line cut of that same drawing, not only because of the closely related quality of book page and drawing paper, but because the physical method of getting ink onto paper by offset is closer to the soft and sensitive touch of brush to paper than is the rigid forcing of an ink-covered metal shape into the fibre of the paper by letterpress printing.

This is also true of work originally done by pen. A good offset reproduction can maintain with great fidelity the original quality of an individual pen line, for example, that starts its stroke with the finest and most delicate of lines, then increases in width and blackness. The inevitable tendency of a letterpress reproduction on book papers of such a line, as all who have struggled with the problem

either as artists or printers know, is for the narrow strip of metal, into which the artist's original pen line has been translated, to be forced far enough into the paper so that the line prints slightly from its sides as well as from its top surface, thus thickening the line and losing the original quality of the artist's work. Because offset prints that line from a flat plate with no difference in height between the part that prints the image and the surrounding white, the factor of thickening through pressure is absent, and the retention of original delicacy and subtlety is thus made possible.

This closeness of the printed work to the physical qualities of the materials with which the artist worked originally is underlined in the area of transparent water color. From the time of the early illuminators of hand-written books on through such great figures as William Blake, there has been a marked affinity on the part of the book artist for water color. Earlier, however, it was impossible to get onto the printed page the special qualities of work in this medium. Offset now makes it possible for book pages to be so planned and produced that

81

they will have . . . the feeling, almost, of the artist's brush itself having been pulled across an area, giving a broken edge of color here, blurring into the still wet paint of another stroke there, leaving the crisp white of the untouched paper to come through elsewhere. This last quality serves a double function in that it produces the original "sparkle" of the medium and at the same time serves as a unifying factor to integrate the illustration with the page. . . .

[The problem of making separations with overlays] was largely circumvented in the making of one of the most original books of recent years for younger children, *See and Say* by Antonio Frasconi. A genuinely creative artist of unique personal vision and great technical resources. Frasconi has achieved a position of unusual distinction in the world of prints in the last dozen years with his work in color woodcut. In developing the pictures for this book of simple words in four languages he worked in exactly the same way by which he produces his complicated color prints for more adult audiences. For every pictorial unit, a separate block of wood was cut for each of the four colors of which it was composed, and these were then inked and printed by hand rubbing. The resulting proof was thus the picture that was to appear on the book page, and because all the elements in its preparation were under the artist's immediate control, any necessary changes or adjustments could be made before proofs of the separate color blocks were made for the offset printer. It is a point of some significance and an indication of the place that offset printing occupies in the world of children's books, that Frasconi's woodcuts, the very medium from which letterpress printing developed, were photographed and printed by offset.

This same way of working, which has some real advantages for the artist, has been utilized by . . . Evaline Ness in her drawings for *The Bridge*. These last, it should be added, were executed as silk-screen prints rather than as woodcuts, but the same principle of complete prior execution of the finished picture by the artist holds true.

Excerpts from the article which appeared in *Illustrators of Children's Books: 1946-1956.*

63. Silk screen illustration by Evaline Ness for *The Bridge* by Charlton Ogburn, Jr., Houghton Mifflin, 1957, 6¼ x 9.

The Artist at Work

In introducing "The Artist at Work" series in the December 1963 Horn Book Magazine, *Ruth Hill Viguers wrote, "This new series is in answer to frequent requests from our readers. The philosophy of the artist's approach has appeared and will continue to be discussed. . . . These articles will deal more specifically with the way his effects are accomplished. We hope this exchange among leading illustrators will be valuable to fellow artists and will help others to be better informed when they look at illustrated books." Articles in the series appeared through the December 1966 issue, and aroused enough interest to be one of the reasons for compiling this volume.*

INTRODUCTION

by Walter Lorraine

It has been said there is art in architecture, but architecture is not art. So, too, with the illustrated book. Here, the picture has a basic literary function that is not necessarily an artistic one. A book illustration is meant to liven, decorate, or explain the text. As in some ways the book is the clothing for the verbal idea, so the picture helps set the style and mood of that clothing. Even the simplest picture by its very nature extends or at least gives new direction to a text.

We think in signs and symbols alluding to the whole. The most graphic verbal description ever written is still incomplete visually; the illustrator has to put in all the connective tissue accurately and appropriately. Because an illustration must show the story situation literally as well as emotionally to be sound in its function, the artist must be able to join the mood and world of the writing as completely as possible. This holds true for picture-book and novel format alike. Whatever the proportion of illustrations to text, their limits are dictated by the idea that is the book.

Since each idea is unique, the illustration must also be unique in forming a complement to the idea. This wedding of text and art is difficult to arrange ideally. Art that serves the function of illustration, yet transcends the mundane to bring a new dimension of experience to the viewer, is not lightly conceived. It can only be born from the individual creative artist's private compulsion. It is not possible to specify as a condition for publication that an author write artistically, nor is it possible to specify that a piece of illustration must be art. It *is* or *is not*, depending on the sensibilities of the artist involved and his response to the text.

Walter Lorraine, Director of Juvenile Books for Houghton Mifflin Company, is experienced as an illustrator and a book designer and also as a production manager of children's books. He has taught book design at the Museum School of Fine Arts in Boston and a typography course at Boston University evening school. Several of the books he has illustrated have been included in the New York Times *annual list of "Ten Best Illustrated Children's Books."*

64. Illustration by Walter Lorraine for *Sir Gawain and the Green Knight* retold by Constance Hieatt, Crowell, 1967.

Often it is said of children's book illustration that the artist must have had fun doing the art. Perhaps he did, or perhaps he did not; this condition is unessential to the act of creating. More often than the fun is the pain of striving for something — a mood, a feeling, a line just beyond one's grasp. The state of the mind at work cannot easily be described.

Facile techniques and tools do not of themselves ensure superior results: a pencil in one hand can be a magic thing, in another nothing but a clumsy stick. Still, as the musical genius is bound by his instrument, so the artist is bound in his expression by medium and techniques. Artistic intent will vary from one artist to another as will what is most appreciated by one viewer or another. For one the excitement will perhaps stem from space-and-movement concepts dependent on flat color and position. As example, red comes forth and blue recedes; and a red edge against a green will vibrate due to their equality of visual impact, because the eye cannot focus clearly on either color. For another artist, a rendered, rounded image with light and shadow in classical perspective may be the form. For example, we learn by experience that the smaller similar object is farther away. These or other sound concepts can be mistreated or sincerely applied with success.

Preparation techniques vary considerably, but are most important only in how well they convey the artist's intent. It is, after all, the printed book that matters. These techniques are in part modes of their age, but also can be stimulations to new art.

At the dawn of printing, the woodcut was the only means of reproducing art. The nonprinting areas were cut away, leaving a raised surface, which when inked and pressed against a piece of paper would duplicate the image — much the same as a fingerprint. Simply speaking, this is what we currently term letterpress.

Through the skills and experimentation of the artists and craftsmen involved, more and more subtle line effects were sought. And so evolved the wood engraving, cut on the end grain of the wood instead of with the grain, as the woodcut. Simulated tone could then be produced through the close spacing of fine lines. If the eye cannot pick out each detailed line, the natural visual response is to mix the line and background to a proportionate gray tone.

Offset lithography grew from stone lithography. . . . Today, instead of stone, metal and more sophisticated chemistry are used. The term "offset" refers to the fact that the original plate never touches the paper; it first impresses onto a so-called "blanket" which becomes the actual printing plate.

65. Pencil drawing by Larry Webster reproduced using a 133-line screen. Circled area in drawing is enlarged to show screen pattern.

During the early years of printing the artist often prepared the printing plates himself. If he did not, a skilled craftsman would copy his art onto the plate. Various methods of carbon-like transfers were sometimes used, but the artist's original sketch rarely could be duplicated line for line until the development of photoengraving. A photograph of the original art was made, and the resulting negative film was then laid directly on the metal plate, the face of which was chemically treated to make it react to light. Light passing through the image areas on the negative hardened the chemical plate surface, leaving it resistant to acid. On exposure to acid, all nonprinting areas were eaten away, leaving the raised printing surface. Artists could now work freely on many different materials with tools more suitable to the individual's taste.

The next major development was the halftone screen. In physical fact this is a grid of lines on glass, so many lines to the linear inch, depending on the desired degree of fineness in the plate, as 75-line screen (approximately that used in news-

papers) or 133-line screen (generally the standard for average reproduction). This grid is positioned between the art and the camera. The art image is broken into a fine dot pattern, the size of the dot giving the degree of tonality (the same visual reaction as for the wood engraving tone). Water color washes and other tonal art techniques could now be reproduced.

Back in the days of the craftsman printer a single plate was often inked by hand with a number of different colored inks; but, since in mechanical reproduction only one color at a time can be printed, full-color painted art could not be reproduced until the development of "camera separated" or "color process" work. Such work incorporated the halftone screen with the introduction of color filters between art copy and camera. In theory, varying tone combinations of the three basic primary colors — red, yellow, and blue — will give a full spectrum range. The filter drew from the art copy, in turn, all the red for one printing plate, all the blue for another, and all the yellow for a third. In most full-color reproduction there is a fourth black plate to give detail and value range.

Essentially, although the processes outlined above are far more sophisticated today, these are the printing techniques at the disposal of the artist. Economic and other factors dictate some art preparation, but theoretically the artist can draw on almost anything with almost any tool in almost any range of colors with some hope of obtaining a reasonable facsimile reproduction.

Preseparated art, where the artist prepares a piece of work for each individual color plate, was created to reduce costs of manufacture by eliminating the expense of color filtering full-color paintings. Today some effects are achieved through preseparated work that could be arrived at in no other way. Using this approach, the artist has unique control over the printed result. Printing has generally improved over the years, even though there has been a loss of personal craftsmanship. The artist who recognizes printing as the mass-production monster it is and works on its terms often obtains most striking results.

The average quality of book illustration in this country today is at a level where it can bear comparison to any time in history. The art movement of the late forties and the fifties that pointed new directions, but brought also a rash of shallow work, has settled down without loss of integrity or progress. There is less superficial copying of an accepted style and more honest individual effort. Time-tested ideas stand equally beside new experiments.

There is, happily, much art in illustration today. It is art that serves well the basic function of illustration yet transcends that function. It stems from the integrity and efforts of many individual creative artists. There is no substitute for appreciating this art other than simply looking at it with an open mind. True art will strike home, and the receiver will be the richer for it.

Excerpts from the article which appeared in *The Horn Book Magazine*, December 1963.

INFLUENCES AND APPLICATIONS
by Leonard Weisgard

. . . From a personal point of view, what is my job as an illustrator?

Apart from the knowledge and proper use of the artist's equipment, it is my job to implement communication, to enhance the word, to extend, provoke, possibly simplify a learning experience that must be pleasurable. It is my job to involve the reader as viewer, sharer, fellow explorer; to dramatize space, integrate the illustration with space and type, the design of which must best suit the particular text's needs. Age level concepts behind the text's thesis must be considered. It is my job to use color or black and white, depending upon budgetary requirements, and to prepare properly the artwork for the mechanical steps of reproducing the illustrations — by line cuts, offset, gravure, letterpress, camera color process, or whatever printing technique has been determined beforehand by the publisher's production department. It is my job to exploit contemporary printing limitations or publishing budgets.

Part of the never-ending training program for any artist is a thorough working knowledge of his equipment, especially the tools he masters. Improvisation and happy accident are often the most rewarding learning experiences that an artist can meet along creative ways. Proust has said, "Creative wrong memory is a source of art."

Shifting styles and changing points of view demand new approaches and techniques in illustration. Such change has even reshaped artist's tools. Work procedures and actual working surfaces are now entirely altered. A resilient and adventurous mind is required to maintain the necessary calm in the face of changes in the field of art supplies alone. Drawing on every source, I have even found that combs are useful to create effects. Painting an undercoat of one color, with an overcoat of another, thickly applied and then combed, will pro-

Although Leonard Weisgard has always worked in many media, his illustrations show a particular sensitivity to the different needs of each text. For his more general observations on children's book illustration, see his article in Section I.

duce striping in a most surprising manner. The jacket and end sheets for Margaret Wise Brown's *The Little Frightened Tiger* (Golden MacDonald, pseud.) had striped bamboo-jungle combed effects as a background for the tiger.

For spatter work and other techniques, I have used toothbrushes, some brushes of camel, badger, or other animal hair, and some of plastic. There is limitless equipment to experiment with, as exciting as any scientist's well-stocked laboratory; flowing pens, some rigid, some flexible, depending upon the quality of line desired; pencils dripping liquid lead, some soft, some hard; and crayons oozing brilliant, burning colors. There are unusual and unlimited surfaces to work on: scratchboard, linoleum, woodblock, tile, tin, etcher's plate, drift or barn wood, lithographer's stone, glass, hot or cold press paper, skin or canvas.

There is the world to choose from. It takes a bright child's stretch of the imagination to realize the possibilities of clothes-, bobby, or cotter pin, paper or diamond clip, welder's torch, metal hanger, ironing board, baking pans and cupcake tins. Put them all together, and you have an artist's studio.

Each book assignment makes different demands. Different demands require different approaches and techniques. In the study of writers as well as of painters, it has been recorded that artist must stand upon artist. Difficult as that position might first appear to be, is this not one way of growing?

A great source of pleasure and inspiration has come to me from the study of the art of the people — folk art, wherever it appears on earth. Long ago graded washes were applied to a bed of velvet or silk, sometimes to transparent glass, as the background for a painting. Then stenciled shapes — grapes, melon, pears, or other fruit — added a contrasting sharpness of edge. Finishing details were painted over all with a controlled but playfully loose manner. Sometimes sandpaper was the background work surface; sometimes sand itself or mica was incorporated into the picture surface, to sparkle fruit bowls or to soften sheep's coats, achieving a *trompe-l'oeil* effect.

Needle with threads of cotton, silk, or wool upon a fabric; needlepoint, hooking with cotton,

rug making, and tapestry have taught me much. Concentrated starings at crisscrossed colored lines, at the light and shadow side of raised wool, have carried me down myriad avenues of further exploration and discovery in painting parallels.

This steeping in folk art is reflected in *Mr. Peaceable Paints*, a book born out of love and respect for the work of the early sign painter. His brilliant contributions to various related trades and fields of applied art I now ardently search for and collect. In the realm of silver work and pewter, Paul Revere was such a craftsman. With *Mr. Peaceable* I had the opportunity for singing the praises of those unsigned creators of weather vanes, inn and trade signs, whirligigs and toys and portraits painted on the run. In the book, pastel chalks, used flat upon a grained surface, provided a background surface to work upon, a background which almost seemed to join in with the artist's. Somewhat the same effect was achieved in early samplers and mourning paintings.

Illustrations for *The Little Island* by Margaret Wise Brown (Golden MacDonald, pseud.) were painted upon pressed wood. Paintings I had seen upon spinets and other musical instruments, on calliope and circus wagons, all contributed to the technique attempted here. First a layer of lead white was applied to the wood, which was then lightly sanded, the aim being to achieve a weathered smoothness. It was my hope that the original sun-drenched vision of an island bathed in predawn golden light could be re-created in morning fresh colors. Adding egg white to tempera seemed to provide a sparkle to the color, heightening the effect. Once I had read that adding egg white to paint was an old trick used by early painters to prepare a *gouache* that would have an opalescence.

Bold shapes, stylized, against grain textured surfaces in Oriental art provided a clue to a technique used for *Where Does the Butterfly Go When It Rains?* by May Garelick. Instead of using wood blocks, I cut paper friskets for the larger shapes. Over grainy board with chalk, color was sponged, allowing undersurfaces to show through. Scratching with a needle added stark white rain lines.

In the Life Long Ago series, the book called *The Athenians in the Classical Period* offered me a

66. Illustration by Leonard Weisgard for *Mr. Peaceable Paints* written and illustrated by Leonard Weisgard, Scribner, 1956, 9½ x 8.

unique opportunity to restudy this period, and I was aided by the trained eye and mind of a man who has actually unearthed, restored, and translated from the artifacts of the earliest Grecian times. Edward Ochsenschlager was a constant guide and check on authenticity.

The thread needed to hold the concept of *The*

Athenians together showed itself quite early in the planning stages. There it is, still remaining on one wall of the Parthenon: the frieze attributed to Phidias, the Procession of the Panathenaic Festival. The strength, beauty, wit and imagination of man's creativity, so wondrously depicted by early Grecian artists, still lives on in their work.

67. Illustration by Leonard Weisgard for *Alice's Adventures in Wonderland and Through the Looking Glass* by Lewis Carroll, Harper, 1949, 8 x 10⅞.

Preparing the pictures for *Alice's Adventures in Wonderland* raised an interesting problem. Tenniel in his time could not use color because printing techniques for that were still to be developed. Throughout all of Lewis Carroll's writing, however, dreamlike textures, sun and shadow light, objects, creatures, people, remembered situations bathed in evocative light call out for color.

Charles Demuth, an American water colorist, had painted fruit in such an evocative manner. His pears insinuated summer fragrance, heat, and insect noise, images of a remembered world that seemed secure, all seen through a hole in a leaf. Another American water colorist, Maurice Prendergast, painted people and scenes, capturing a tapestry mood, but his technique suggested color dropped in happy puddles. Two Frenchmen, lithographers, painters, and illustrators, both had completely beguiled me with their work. Bonnard and Vuillard achieved an extraordinary quality of design in everything they did. Their work evokes fresh and contradictory feelings side by side, a Sunday-stillness feeling fraught with significant waiting.

Studying and admiring the work of these painters, holding love and respect in my heart and head for what they had achieved, I began to experiment, keeping their qualities in the forefront of my mind. From all the experiments and attempts a technique evolved.

Because I enjoy space so, the illustrations for *Alice* were prepared larger than actual size, later reduced by camera to the book size. Before I approach any job of illustrating, before I put pencil to paper, I must see and know what is in my mind's eye. I must see it all, picture by picture, in my head. Once I have seen, the execution will flow faster.

A large drawing table was cleared, paraphernalia placed nearby, convenient and ready when needed: jars, water, rags, brushes, scissors, blotters, and so on. Because the summer heat caused rapid drying, the first part of the operation required speed. *Gouache* and water color were loaded heavily on the brush, and I applied this thickly to established blocked-out areas. Lightly penciled guidelines charted the course. Already wet sections of the illustration board allowed the color to wriggle, making squirming patterns. Then with freshly washed and ironed sheeting, scrunched together to fit the full hand, I daubed at certain areas. With clean white blotting paper I daubed at others. The sheeting picked up excess pigment, leaving a patternization of the sheeting, suggesting light showing through color. With a blotter, other color areas were textured by blotting lightly, again picking up excess pigment.

Japanese stencil brushes were used in still other areas to pile color onto color and then to diminish out towards the edges for foliage effects. I relish painting things over things, even if you can't see what is beneath. I know it is there and it gives me pleasure — as a secret world. A set designer does much the same thing; in creating a backdrop he places objects in front and people before it all. I enjoy knowing that there is a leaf beneath another leaf, and moths and butterflies over them; as in nature there is always something else, something behind, above, and below. As in thinking, one thought leads to another, one obliterating, one engulfing another.

Today's illustrator often attempts to achieve the level of accomplishment that the unself-conscious child attains naturally and artlessly in his own work. Unless an illustrator has a special talent based upon sound draftsmanship and a complete knowledge and understanding of his craft, however, he cannot achieve honest and joyous communication and a sense of freedom with any other human. It is not so simple as just drawing or painting or creating as the child does.

In the beginning and in the end, our senses are perhaps more honest than intelligence is, and nothing is more real than the "first" of all experiences. Of all the organs, the eye is the most easily infatuated, then jaded, and so tricked. Seeing is sometimes pleasure, sometimes pain, but not necessarily knowledge. But through the experience of art we can gain an insight into what it means to be free in emotional response and free in the choice of ideas — free in a world that is still filled with beauty.

Excerpts from the article which appeared in *The Horn Book Magazine*, August 1964.

COLLAGE

by Ezra Jack Keats

Although collage is considered a new art form, it can be traced to humble beginnings, as far back as a century ago, probably more. Homemade picture books for children were created by cutting out patterns and pictures from old magazines, newspapers, and any other sources available. The cutouts were pasted on blank sheets, arranged in story sequences, and made into books. Many children the world over still have fun making books this way. In its contemporary form, artistic considerations have entered to give collage its high aesthetic value. Its name derived from the French verb *coller*, "to paste," at about the turn of the century. Among its famous exponents of the time were the cubists Braque, Picasso, and Gris, who had joined artists from all corners of the world in Paris to share their views on art. In his last years Matisse adopted a variation of collage and also used it as a method of designing the vestments and stained-glass windows for the famous chapel at Vence, France. Today collage appears in advertising, magazine, and book illustration.

According to my dictionary, collage is made by "employing various materials, such as newspaper clippings, fragments of advertising, etc., with lines and color supplied by the artist." So it is — and more. But before elaborating on the technique, I would like to discuss its character: what it has in common with other art forms, and what distinguishes it from other art forms.

All painting is a delicate balance between illusion and reality. A painting may present a subject in which the viewer perceives great distances and solid three-dimensional forms. Both the painter and the viewer are aware, however, that the distances and solid forms are, in reality, only on a flat surface. One of the prerequisites of aesthetic excitement is the mutual acceptance of this phenomenon. The painter invites the viewer to imagine that the trees he painted are solid, that the fields on which the trees stand roll far into the distance, and that the sky is space extending into infinity. He may utilize perspective, advancing or receding colors, and other means; but everything occurs on a flat surface, and the viewer participates with the artist in the act of creating the scene.

Collage is distinguished from other art forms in that its *harmonious fusion of independent shapes and colors* makes for a more unusual balance between illusion and reality. For instance, a pattern that has its own character, when used in combina-

tion with other patterns, becomes something else.

Some of the pictures in *The Snowy Day* are examples of this. A decorative paper becomes a room; flat shapes of color and designs become buildings, snow, a pillow, pajamas on a boy, and so on. There is no shading on the pajamas or the linen to make them look solid, nor is there any delineation between the sleeve and the body. No definition of line or shading shows where the pillow meets the bed, nor is the edge of the bed cover defined. The viewer makes it round, gives it space, follows the implications. (In a few instances, for special reasons, more definition is introduced, such as in Peter's face.) If I were painting the sky behind the snow hill, I would try to design some interesting clouds on a blue sky. But here the patterned paper offered me a unique possibility.

As for the technique, the tools — in addition to the conventional ones, such as pencils, brushes, paint, and ink — are scissors, tweezers, razor blades, cutting knives, rubber cement, glue, sponges, burnishers, colored and patterned papers (some have been sent to me by interested readers), ink rollers, tooth brushes for spattered effects, stencils, and gum erasers from which shapes are cut to be used as stamps.

The edges of shapes are varied in several ways. Sharp edges are made by cutting; rough edges by tearing; soft edges by painting over them.

The artist is unconcerned that the overlapping sheets of paper showing through, or the edges casting shadows, reveal an illustration to be composed of pasted paper and other materials. If anything, this obvious superimposition is an integral part of the character of the medium, as are, for instance, the thick impasto strokes in oil painting.

There are also strange and unpredictable situations. What could be a minor disaster can turn out to be a pleasant surprise. Sometimes when all the materials have been cut out, composed, and are ready to paste, a careless movement of one's arm will sweep everything on the page into a frightful state — or into a new arrangement suggesting a composition one never would have thought of.

The nature of collage demands new means of expression from the artist. In *Whistle for Willie*, the sequel to *The Snowy Day*, the hero of the book,

Ezra Jack Keats is self-taught. He showed artistic ability at an early age, but preferred to motivate his own development and evolving styles. Before breaking into the children's book field, he painted murals, posters, and magazine illustrations. The first book for which he used collage was The Snowy Day, *which was awarded the 1963 Caldecott Medal.*

When he stopped
everything turned
down . . .
and up . . .

and up . . .
and down . . .
and around
and around.

68. Illustration by Ezra Jack Keats for *Whistle for Willie* written and illustrated by Ezra Jack Keats, Viking, 1964, 9 x 8.

Peter, has been turning in circles and becomes dizzy. How to illustrate this? First there was the temptation to draw the often-used swirling ellipses around him. But to keep the illustration in the realm of collage, I decided to make the sky appear agitated by changing it from a solid to a marbleized pattern. On the next page I tilted the composition up, and on the following page I tilted it down. To increase the feeling of dizziness, I had the traffic lights appear to be floating about in mid-air!

The ratio between the use of painting and drawing and the use of collage should be determined according to the judgment of the illustrator with every new book. Each new manuscript presents a challenge and an adventure; and I look forward to applying this technique in fresh and appropriate ways.

From *The Horn Book Magazine*, June 1964.

WOODCUT ILLUSTRATION

by Evaline Ness

Wood is beautiful. All kinds of wood. I like to look at it. I like to smell it and feel it. Most of all, I like to cut it. No matter how well-planned my design may be, when once it has been transferred to wood, cut and printed, it is enhanced with a lovely quality which I could never produce by my own hand.

The Chinese must have felt the same way. They were printing from wood blocks in the ninth century. The Europeans got around to it much later — at the beginning of the fifteenth century.

When once I have decided that a particular story "needs" the bold simplicity of woodcut illustrations, I go to the lumberyard. There are many

Evaline Ness did not begin studying art until after she had been to a teacher's college. She attended the Chicago Art Institute, planning to be a fashion artist. Her first illustrations were for Seventeen *magazine. Eventually she did book jackets and then picture books, some of which she also wrote. One of these,* Sam, Bangs and Moonshine, *won the 1967 Caldecott Medal.*

woods to choose from: cherry, lime, maple, syca-more, bass, white pine, redwood, mahogany. They are all good woods for cutting, neither too hard nor too soft. A hard wood (like oak) is difficult to cut, and a soft wood refuses fine detail work and might break down in the printing process. But no matter what wood is selected it should be well seasoned and dry. Plywood can be used also, but it has lim-itations: because the grain of each layer of wood runs in the opposite direction to the ones next to it, the cutting is unpleasant and hard to control. I generally use it for underprinting large simple areas. Masonite can be used, too, but it is lifeless compared to wood.

I prefer white pine, knots and all. Knots have changed my design from mediocrity to excitement. They have given me an entirely original idea for a design.

At the lumberyard I have the wood cut into blocks of the page size that I will use throughout the book. When the blocks are in my studio, I first rub them with steel wool to bring up the grain. After that I "wash" them with a thin coat of brown or blue watered ink so that I can see clearly the cuts as I make them. Then my design goes on the block.

Sometimes I draw directly on the block with brush and ink. Other times I transfer my design with carbon paper, being very careful not to bear down on the pencil too much. Most woods are much more sensitive and soft than is generally realized. The tip of a fingernail can make a dent. If I have used the transfer method, I blacken all areas which I want to remain. In other words, I cut wood away from the positive image.

There are dozens of cutting tools on the market. I have settled on five. One Japanese knife for sharp clean edges. One scrive (a V-shaped hollow burin). Two hollow rounded gouges — one fine, one large. The fifth tool is an electric drill for quickly clearing away unwanted background.

After the tools, there are infinite possibilities for making texture in wood by pounding, gluing, and scratching. Nails, screws, paper clips, wire mesh or anything else which will make a dent are for pounding. Cloth, textured paper, veneers, caning, even leaves can be glued to wood. These should always be coated with shellac. As for scratching, even a pin can be used.

But no matter what tool I may be using, I do not follow my design slavishly. The feeling of cutting

69. Illustration by Evaline Ness for *Josefina February* written and illustrated by Evaline Ness, Scribner, 1963, 7⅜ x 10.

Not long ago on a high hill in Haiti there lived a little girl named Josefina February. Josefina lived with her grandfather, Mr. February, in a house that had one room, bamboo walls and a banana leaf roof.

is completely different from drawing. I try to let the wood medium express itself.

If the book I am illustrating has two or more colors, I always cut the black plate first. It is the key plate. When that has been done, I roll out printer's ink on a glass palette with a gelatin brayer. When the brayer is completely covered, it is rolled gradually on the block until all raised surfaces shine evenly with ink.

The paper I use for printing is a thin Japanese mending tissue. I cut a piece larger than the block and carefully lay it on the inked surface. With a wooden Japanese rice spoon, I start rubbing, section by section, until the imprint can clearly be seen on the reverse side. Then I hold my breath, lift one corner of the paper, and gently peel it back and off the block in one movement. The first proof! Everything is wrong. Everything is exciting. There are things to correct by more cutting. There are things to be left; thrilling unexpected things. Bless wood.

Eventually, when the black plate is finished, it is inked and rubbed off, this time on wax paper. The wax-paper image is placed face down on another block and rubbed off. There is my design on wood ready for cutting the color design which will overlay it. And so on to the third and fourth block, depending on how many colors are used. Here is where plywood or other textures can be used to give a fillip to subject matter which has been straight cutting.

Since most picture books are done on overlays (cheaper printing process than full color) each of my color plates is printed in black, the color being designated for the printer. I keep the actual colors before me as I work. I hum. I imagine the result. I see it all. It is perfect.

The day comes when the publisher sends me the printed book. Everything is wrong. It is not what I had expected. There are glaring mistakes too late to correct. I decide to change my career. (How could anything go wrong, say, if one were a berry-picker?) But before I do, I take one more look at the book, page by page. The thrilling unexpected things are still there. Bless wood.

From *The Horn Book Magazine*, October 1964.

CARDBOARD CUTS

by Blair Lent

"How does the printing surface last for ten thousand printings?"

"It doesn't," I answered. "It would only last for about one hundred good impressions!"

The visitor to my studio, who was unfamiliar with book production, had watched me make a cut, ink it, and then print from the cut onto a sheet of paper. He thought that I had actually prepared a printing plate for the printer. He may even have thought I was printing the book!

There was a time when the artist, or a craftsman who copied the artist's original drawing, did make a woodcut or a wood engraving to be used on the printing press. Contemporary printers print from metal or chemical surfaces. The plates have been mechanically reproduced from photographs of the illustrator's original artwork. A very few limited editions are printed today from woodcuts — but I don't even make a woodcut!

A cardboard cut resembles a wood, or linoleum, cut except that a thin, less permanent material is used. A few years ago, I would often experiment with a design on cardboard before starting a woodcut. One day I was satisfied with the effects from the cardboard itself. I haven't used wood since.

Cardboard is less resistant than wood or linoleum. It is an ideal material for illustration because my ideas are realized much sooner. Large areas of cardboard that are not to be printed can be cut around and removed with a single motion. There is flexibility in working this way; I can cut up several cardboard cuts and re-assemble them. Several textures of cardboard may be combined in one print. The natural pattern of wood grain is missing,

Blair Lent studied at the Museum School of Fine Arts, Boston, and in Europe on a traveling scholarship. While he submitted stories and illustrations to publishers without success, he supported himself by doing art for advertisements. After his first book, Pistachio, *was accepted for publication, his illustration began winning honors in the children's book field.* The Wave *by Margaret Hodges was a Caldecott Honor Book in 1965; with his illustration for* The Funny Little Woman, *retold by Arlene Mosel, he won the 1973 Caldecott Medal.*

but I have found several varieties of cardboard with their own interesting surfaces.

Overcoming the material's limitations can be stimulating. Cardboard is a fragile and somewhat primitive material to work with, but the more I work with cardboard the more I discover that what has been impossible is possible.

Supplies are basic and easy to get. The only equipment I need is medium-weight cardboard, single-edged razor blades, ink, and paper.

I have simplified my procedure, but it still does seem odd — to make a printing surface, print it, and send the print to the printer, who will turn the artwork into a printing surface a second time and then print the design again! The quality of line that I get when I print, however, is much more interesting than if I were to draw directly on illustration board. The spontaneity necessary for the finished illustration is not eliminated. In fact, I am less self-conscious about my finished design because I know that the print will have a character of its own. The only trouble is that my studio becomes littered with little pieces of cardboard; they stick to my clothes and track into other people's houses.

The cutting takes much less time than the preparation. By the time my sketches are transferred to the cardboard, my illustrations have been pretty well realized.

Most of the books I illustrate require research. I wish that I could go to Japan or Arabia, to Mexico, Russia, or the South Seas to sketch because the books that I have been working on take place there. But a trip to the library and a vicarious journey through *The National Geographic* are more within my budget. Research may influence not only the book that I am working on at the time, but the books that follow. Architectural details, costumes, and unfamiliar plant life will affect my design.

Enthusiastic preliminary sketches seem to take no time at all. The most difficult step is the final development of the characters. I worked for days (perhaps weeks) to try to create the right green cow for *Pistachio*. I wanted her to look like a lovable stuffed toy; for, after all, she is not a real cow — she can ride a bicycle and dance on the tightwire with a polka-dot umbrella. The cardboard cuts that I eventually made for this book were bold, in the manner of a circus poster.

Another book, *Oasis of the Stars* by Olga Economakis, was developed in a different way. Mrs. Economakis has written about the desert and the difficult life there. The camels do not dance, they work hard; they are more literally illustrated than the green cow.

Tada, a Japanese boy in *The Wave* by Margaret Hodges, is tiny, seemingly porcelain, against the almost overwhelming forces of nature. The Japanese village is detailed and fragile. A tidal wave lifts the houses from the soil and carries them away. The wave is powerful and cut with only a few strokes.

When the characters look as much like the author's words as I can make them, I begin to put together a rough dummy that will correspond to the finished book. After discussing the dummy with the editor and the art director, I am ready to start on the cardboard cuts.

I make a tracing of each sketch in the dummy with a soft lead pencil, and the tracing is rubbed on its reverse side onto the cardboard. A spray of pastel fixative keeps the transferred pencil lines from smudging when I begin to cut.

Laminated cardboard, manufactured with about eight layers of heavy paper, is best suited for my work. With a single-edged razor blade I cut out areas that I do not want to print. The material is peeled away. If I want a texture to print from a negative area, I will peel away only a few layers of paper. If I want no ink to print at all, I will peel away about five layers. Delicate lines are incised with the points of the blade. Since the cardboard dulls the cutting edge of the blades very fast, I may use ten or fifteen razor blades for one illustration.

Sometimes I use a safety pin. For *Oasis of the Stars*, I tapped a pin into the cardboard to make nearly thirty-two pages of texture to represent sand. Neighbors in the apartment below could hear the slight, repeated vibrations through their ceiling. They asked me what I was doing. I told them that I was making sand; and when, later on, I had finished, I made one grand thump as a final statement.

I do not always appear to be working on an assembly line, however. For the same book I enjoyed

95

cutting an intricate design to print as an Oriental rug. The cut made a pattern on the cardboard that reminded me of the printing blocks made in India for decorating fabrics. Most of the time, though, the cardboard cuts — one piece of gray cardboard after another — look uninteresting. They come to life on my printing press.

After a cardboard cut is finished, I shellac it. The shellac protects the cardboard; otherwise it would deteriorate from the ink that I will apply.

I brush block-printing ink onto the raised surfaces of the cardboard. I do not use a roller because I want the brush marks to show. I also like to control the amount of ink applied to each part of the design. Sometimes I brush the cardboard cut with ink that is almost dry. Other times I add turpentine to the ink. I also vary the paper that I print on; one variety may absorb the ink, another may repel it. I use a small sixteen-by-twenty-inch hand-pressure press, and may make as many as twenty-five impressions from one cardboard cut.

I study the assortment of prints for each illustration and then scissor the most interesting parts

from them. For a typical illustration in *The Wave*, the sea was taken from a blotty print. The village on the shore, on the same page, was chosen from a print that had been printed with a drier ink. This step would have been impossible for the early illustrator; his woodcuts were printed when the book went to press, and his illustrations were uniformly inked.

I hope, after all the cutting, tapping, brushing, and blotting, that I have completed a picture book with some vitality. The harmony of the illustration and the story is what matters, regardless of the method, whether it be from a cardboard cut or a lithograph stone, or just drawn with the stub of a pencil.

Technique, design, and color are part of the illustrator's language; they are to be mastered, but more important, the book should offer something for a child to experience and enjoy. My manner of working may seem involved to the visitor to my studio, but my objective is the same as another illustrator with a more direct approach: to make a good book.

From *The Horn Book Magazine*, August 1965.

70. Illustration by Blair Lent for *The Wave* by Margaret Hodges, Houghton Mifflin, 1964, 9¼ x 9.

"A tidal wave!" shrieked the people. And then all shrieks and all sounds and all power to hear sounds were ended by a shock heavier than any thunder, as the great wave struck the shore with a weight that sent a shudder through the hills.

COLOR SEPARATION

by Adrienne Adams

Confronted with a new story, I often have a sinking sensation. Accepting it, months ago, seemed so easy; at that time I was in the middle of another story and was only concerned with finding that I *liked* this one, not with "seeing" the illustrations; or if I could "see" them tentatively, then, I have somehow lost the vision and suddenly, now, it looks formidable. My mind is a blank.

Now I do what experience has taught me and read the story over and over, very slowly, at the pace of reading to a child. At perhaps the fifth reading I begin to "see" it, and I feel better.

With scissors I cut up the galley-proof sheets. I scotch-tape the pieces into the pages of an exact-size dummy. I work with it until everything 'fits'; the turning of a page regulates the time and paces it. The picture space gives a chance to enlarge on and augment the story. For some inexplicable reason, I love this part of bookmaking; I have infinite patience with it and do not mind how long the process is.

I am told that it is sometimes a help to a writer, on beginning a story, to put into one sentence what the story is all about, to state its theme in a few words. Similarly, I find it a help, as an illustrator, to turn next to the making of a quick thumbnail sketch of the book — a little four-by-five-inch dummy — in color. It gives me something to depart from, at the least. The editor enjoys seeing the dummy too. At this point there is an easy give-and-take between us; my point of view has not become set. I now have the impetus to plunge in, deeper, and to get at the job I have been fretting over and delaying.

As I return to the full-sized dummy, I must keep in mind the restrictions based on decisions made earlier by the editor and me, technical and economic restrictions, which fence me in. How the book is to be printed, and what the method for preparing the art work for reproduction will be, were decided at the outset. These fences do not bother me; so long as I accept them from the beginning and work within them.

I have used several methods in the making of books: line drawings, or line plus flat-area illustrations that can be reproduced by means of line engravings; pencil drawings on Dinobase, a sand-blasted acetate used in the "direct process," which I will not try to define here; full-color illustrations for offset-lithography reproduction, where the camera is used to separate the colors; and full-color illustration where the artist himself does the separating.

I have decided to discuss the last method because it is the most difficult for me. I use it only when a story seems to push me in that direction, and also because I have a natural inclination toward water-color illustrations.

The hope of the illustrator is that he will be able to retain control of the elements of his design in its transfer to book page through the hands of the craftsmen who separate it into its parts and put it together again on the printed sheet.

If the separating out of these elements (the four colors, black, red, yellow, and blue) is to be done by the artist, he must, as he does an illustration, keep in mind how he is going to undo it. He must present to the bookmaker not one drawing, but four — one for each color — so that when they are printed, one on top of another (stacked, you might say), the picture is put back together again and resembles the original.

In camera-separated work, this job is done by the camera through the use of filters; it is very costly, and not so accurate as you would suppose. When the job is done by the artist, it is painfully tedious. A big risk is that one can become bored, and, getting involved in details, lose sight of the whole.

Despite the hazards, I have wanted to work in water colors enough to take a chance when, for instance, I made the little book about a Maine island, *The Light in the Tower*, and again in *Houses from the Sea*. I could not see doing shells and water in

Adrienne Adams began free-lancing as a commercial artist, doing displays, murals, and decorative textiles, but soon turned to the children's book field. She has now illustrated many books, some written by her husband, John Lonzo Anderson, and some by other authors. She has illustrated two Caldecott Honor Books: Houses from the Sea, *1960, and* The Day We Saw the Sun Come Up, *1962, both written by Alice E. Goudy.*

pencil on Dinobase with the resulting grainy look, or with line cut and its flat effect. But what method to use? It is easy enough in a book like *What Makes a Shadow?* to make a flat drawing for each color — very much like playing with a simple jigsaw puzzle; and when one has designed for it, the results can be satisfying.

In separating wash paintings for halftone reproduction, I am dealing with overlapping gradations of the four different colors to achieve many other colors. I begin with the shades of black, my most important color, for it tells most of the story. I mentally select out all that is black in my painting and, calling this my key drawing, do it on illustration board. Then — on acetate, so that I can see through to the key drawing — I do a painting of only the red areas. With scotch tape I hinge the red drawing on the left of the key drawing so that I can fold it back out of the way when I do the blue drawing, which I hinge from the top. Then comes the yellow drawing, hinged on the right. One can easily see that it would be cumbersome if all were hinged from the same side, for when working on the top one I would have to view the key drawing through three thicknesses of acetate instead of one.

I take care of the exact fitting of one drawing over another by the use of register marks $\oplus$, which can be bought, printed on acetate adhesive tape. These help the platemaker too, and they can be removed before the printing stage arrives.

The real stumper, and the part that is difficult to explain without demonstrating, is this: each separated color-painting is done by me in tones of black so that it will photograph better and make a truer plate. Everyone knows that blue photographs weak, red photographs strong. If I do each painting in black, I can keep to truer values. Of course, each plate will be printed in its intended color of ink.

The transfer, in my mind, of (for instance) the yellow areas to black is a difficult problem. For each of the colors it is difficult. As a tool to aid me here I use the Coloron graduated transparencies of printer's inks. The Process colors are my selection. On these Coloron acetate sheets are printed ten bars of a given color, from 10%, 20%, 30% on up to 100% value of that color. Since these are on acetate, I can lay the yellow transparent sheet over the blue sheet, and by moving the yellow sheet around over the varying percentages of blue arrive

at the green I have used in the grass area, for instance, of my original painting. It is 30% blue and 90% yellow, I may find. I analyze my whole painting so, lightly writing in the little computations all over the original. When I make the yellow separation, knowing the grass must be 90% yellow, I now paint in 90% black, for at hand I have the Coloron acetate sheet for the gradations of black to guide me.

Such effort does not guarantee precise results. One must consciously design with the hazards in mind. Keep it casual, free. Let the colors overlap carelessly; if a design is very carefully made, the error will stand out like a sore thumb. If many areas are loosely put together, one's eye accepts the looseness in its entirety.

I did not follow my own advice when I did *Butterfly Time*. I dared to try to separate butterflies exactly, I will shy away from another challenge like that one; but I did fall in love with the butterflies, and so pushed on, getting terribly involved in the minutest details. Have you ever observed the marbleized underside of the wings of a Painted Lady? Or a Red Admiral? Attempting to separate the elements into overlapping color areas was madness. I was able to find and buy specimens of these beautiful but elusive creatures so that I could hold and turn and study them. When I got home and discovered the tiny labels on the pins supporting them, I was filled with doubt; the Great Spangled Fritillary had been caught in 1937! How true could its colors be — had they faded greatly? Almost immediately I saw two Fritillaries in our yard. I followed them and knew that mine was just as rich in color as the living ones. And then I saw a Red Admiral; I could have caught it had I not one, just as brilliant, on a pin, captured eighteen years before.

It is far more reasonable, and simpler, to separate the colors for a fable or fairy tale. Any color I have used is arbitrarily chosen. It need register as perfectly as possible and be pleasing to the eye. That is all.

The illustration for the following color pages, printed by preseparated art, was prepared by Adrienne Adams to illustrate her use of separations and the carefully planned use of process colors in making these separations.

71. Key drawing of black areas done on white illustration board with pencil line, grey wash, and strong blacks and whites.

72. Artist's separation in black for magenta (red) areas.

73. The plate printed in magenta (red).

74. Artist's separation in black for yellow areas.

75. The plate printed in yellow.

76. Artist's separation in black for cyan (blue) areas.

77. The plate printed in cyan (blue).

78, 79. Progressive proofs are made to see if any correction in color is needed.

Most of what I have said here has had to do with the real *chore* part of bookmaking. I thought it might be the least well-known part and not uninteresting. Every kind of work we do has its tougher, trying moments. To balance, here, I could mention a higher moment. It does not come, as you might think, when I hold the finished book in my hand and find my effort was all so very worth while. I never feel so. I have regrets, then, that I cannot do the book over.

Rather, the moment is that one of optimistic new hope I feel as I begin the next one — hope that now, given another chance, I will do a *better* book.

From *The Horn Book Magazine*, April 1964.

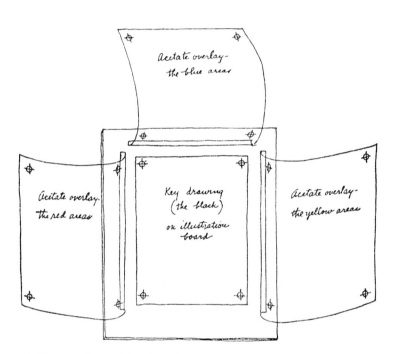

80. Diagram of assembling the artist's acetate separations. Hinging of the acetates (see text) is for the convenience of the artist; the bookmaker takes the arrangement apart to photograph it.

81. Illustration as achieved by preseparated art.

COLOR SEPARATION: THE USE OF PHOTOSTATS

by Juliet Kepes

When I was asked . . . to write an article for the Artist at Work series about the method I use for illustrating my books, I found myself in somewhat of a quandary. The genesis of a book is not an orderly process, at least for me, and consequently it is difficult to trace a book's growth in an orderly way.

I try to tackle a book, from the beginning of the idea to its final realization, as an indivisible whole — text, drawing, and production. To follow the steps I take would be like leading the reader through an imaginary maze, for I continually change direction. I shall try to diagram the process so that I can give some picture of the meanderings that lead to a finished book. Perhaps the stages of the journey will be more meaningful if I take as a concrete example *Lady Bird, Quickly*.

I had first to develop the theme, which in the beginning I wrote down as rapidly as possible while the ideas were pouring out. The story, taking on workable form, had to be whittled and shaped, cut and added to. During this process I made little sketches for the illustrations in the margins and on scraps of paper. I then had to consider what I wanted to express in the drawings, the colors I would use, the layout, jacket, and end papers, and everything else needed for the production of a book except the final printing and binding. I ran into many blind alleys before reaching final decisions.

When I had arrived at some idea as to how much text I would use on a page — that is, made up my mind about the relative proportion between text and illustration, the story sequence and the probable positions of pictures and text — I had galleys made in the type face I had chosen.

While the galleys were being prepared I bound together sheets for a dummy to indicate the layout.

Juliet Kepes grew up in England and attended Brighton School of Art in England and the School of Design in Chicago. Galleries and museums in the United States have exhibited her work, and Lady Bird, Quickly *was a* New York Herald Tribune *Spring Festival Honor Book.*

Using different techniques to determine which would be the most appropriate, I made many sketches in pencil on a rough surface, in pen on a smooth surface, and with brush on Japanese and watercolor paper. In the end, some drawings done with black crayon on charcoal paper pleased me. The paper was too delicate for the many handlings that it would have to go through during the course of the work; therefore, I had the drawings photostated. An advantage in using photostats is that they can be made in both positive and negative, and I planned to use the negative prints for the last pages of the night illustrations, thus avoiding the necessity of having to reverse them by hand. Then I began to prepare the color separations. From the black and white photostats of the line drawings, I traced the areas I would use for each color. These tracings were then transferred onto illustration boards. Using a set of gray-gradation paints, I began painting the areas in the percentages of color to be used. Continually checking a color chart, I selected the gray values to approximate as closely as I could the values of the final colors. This is a very tricky operation, as one has to compare the values over and over, keeping in mind a standard gray scale. I continued this painstaking task for each color separation on each page, as indicated in the sketches.

The red and yellow plates were alike in that both were of an even percentage of color on the same areas, allowing me to use the one plate for both. Rather than fill in the whole background for the indication of color, it was easier to block out the forms not to be red and yellow and then reverse the plate.

Of course the simplest and safest way of doing all this is to have color separations made photographically by the engraver directly from the artist's original painted or colored illustrations, but most publishers consider this an expensive method for reproducing illustrations. One could still cut down on some of the tedious work by using transparent acetates to prepare the color separations. I decided not to use them for this particular book because I hoped to have strong, rich colors with practically no shadings. It has been my experience that good flat color areas cannot be painted on acetates because the paint tends to run and flow into puddles and uneven values and the edges of the painted

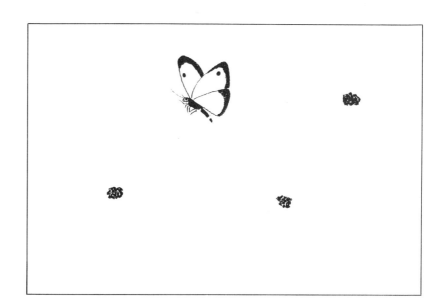

82. Preseparated art for *Lady Bird, Quickly* — black plate.

83. Preseparated art for *Lady Bird, Quickly* — red and yellow plate. In this case (see text) the plate for both the red and the yellow happens to be exactly the same.

84. Preseparated art for *Lady Bird, Quickly* — blue plate.

areas collect into a dark outline. This does not rule out the use of acetates, however, for they can be an excellent method for some effects and can be combined very successfully with other techniques. I regret to say that in the method I chose, and even with the use of acetates for separations, there is a great loss in the quality of the line drawings. For by the very act of having to do the careful copies for separations, repeating shapes and areas where color is indicated, much of the life and freshness of the lines is lost. Nevertheless, when the plates were finished in the black, white, and grays, I found them so attractive that I reserved an idea to do a book just this way sometime — that is, without translating it into color at all.

After I had handed in the completed work for *Lady Bird, Quickly*, I was on tenterhooks for the ages it seems to take before a book is printed. I could hardly wait to know how successful I had been in my judgments about the color and just how accurate in the registering of all the tracings and separations.

When I finally received the printed book, I was almost afraid to open it. After I had mustered up enough courage to look through the work I had spent so much thought on for so many months, I was relieved and delighted with the way the colors had come out. This is the great moment.

From *The Horn Book Magazine*, December 1965.

85. Illustration as achieved by preseparated art for *Lady Bird, Quickly* written and illustrated by Juliet Kepes, Atlantic, 1964, 6 x 9.

to bright-colored butterfly,

28

And, deeper in the jungle, beyond the pool,
where it was quiet and dark and peaceful,
the little boy found a sleeping lion and a sleeping tiger,
and a small jungle cat
asleep under a bush.

86. Illustration by Dahlov Ipcar for *The Calico Jungle* written and illustrated by Dahlov Ipcar, Knopf, 1965, 7⅝ x 11.

COMBINING DINOBASE AND WASH ON PAPER

by Dahlov Ipcar

When Dinobase first appeared on the scene, some years back, it was greeted with enthusiasm. Illustrators, who had tried to hold down costs by doing flat or "line" work for reproduction, now felt they would be able to achieve three-dimensional "shaded" work equal to color lithography. This was something of an illusion, for Dinobase is actually very disappointing as a lithographic medium. It lacks the fine, subtle grain of stone or even zinc, and the results are apt to have a very

For Dahlov Ipcar's remarks about her self-training in the arts, see Section II.

"crayonny" look. A certain amount of this effect was charming, but there was so much of it that it became trite. And the quality of the work suffered. As anyone who has worked with children's art classes knows, crayons can be the most feeble and least colorful of all the art materials that children use.

Before Dinobase came along, my separations were done on paper in ink, using many dry-brush effects, or on Copyrite "stippo" 010 (another plastic with a grained surface). But although one could use litho crayon on these mediums for shading, much of the shading was lost in reproduction. Therefore, I tried to keep my artwork fairly flat, using very little crayon.

Working on Dinobase I have used more crayon and done more shading; but I still do not like to use crayon over large areas. It is most satisfactory when the shading is underlaid with a different flat color. I like the effect of large, simple areas of color, and my style is generally a compromise between flat and three-dimensional.

The selection of colors for a book is fascinating but heart-breaking because one is so limited — usually to four colors at most. Since there are so many subtleties of color that cannot be achieved with just four colors (and one of them black, of course), I try to pick colors that will overlap to make another quite distinctive color. In this way one gets more richness out of a limited palette.

The only trouble with flat color is that it is *so* flat. It lacks tonal subtlety. I always do color comprehensives or "comps" before starting my separations; sometimes I do a pretty rough job on them, but just the random shading that the brush strokes give, even when carelessly applied, makes the comps much livelier and freer looking than the finished, flat printed color.

Lately I have been using a combination of Dinobase and water color paper in my separations in order to capture some of this elusive freshness. One can get lovely effects with water color wash on paper, but of course the reproduction has to be done in halftone. I have found that if I do one color separation as a halftone on paper and the other colors on Dinobase the final result retains much of the liveliness that might otherwise be lost. Even the Dinobase crayonny shading seems to blend in more subtly. I always do the halftone with black water color paint, but in the final printing I prefer that the halftone be one of the colors other than black. A black halftone over everything gives a three-dimensional look to the pictures, but also tends to gray everything down; and a really three-dimensional effect is not something I like.

The water color paper has to be of fairly heavy weight (I use 72-lb. Strathmore paper) to prevent its buckling too much when wet. But it cannot be completely opaque, as I do all my separations on a light table. I do the painting on paper first and then fasten the Dinobase to it layer by layer, taping each sheet down securely as I go along, so that nothing moves. This makes for more accurate registration in the end. (When working entirely on Dinobase one can check the registration by turning the pile over and looking through the plastic from the other side.) I note changes with a pencil on the bottom of the first sheet; then as I peel off the layers, I can make minor corrections, erasing the pencil marks in the end.

I have never used more than two sheets of Dinobase plus one sheet of paper. This makes a three-color job (four colors should be possible, but registration might suffer). Books I have done this way are *Black and White* and *I Love My Anteater with an A.* I also used the halftone on paper for the two-color spreads of . . . *The Calico Jungle.* In this case, however, I used flat poster-paint grays on the halftone pages rather than washes because I wanted a very flat effect. The four-color spreads were done entirely on Dinobase for the same reason.

The Calico Jungle was inspired by collages that I made out of fabrics with bright, small, calico-like designs. I copied the collage effect in paint. Both a problem and a delight of this book was translating the fabric effect into flat color. I designed literally hundreds of small prints simple enough to reproduce with pen and ink.

Not really pen, for actually almost all my drawing is done with a fine sable-hair brush rather than a pen. I draw more freely and surely with a brush. On Dinobase, I also use pencils: plain lead pencils for delicate lines, and two kinds of wax pencils for shading, soft (Eagle Prismacolor black 935) and hard (Eagle "chemi-sealed" Verithin black 747). Some artists work with colored pencils on Dinobase, and with a light table they can see approximately how the colors will look when combined. But this gives only a very rough idea of the final result, and I soon abandoned the method. Dinobase acts as its own film for reproduction, and I find that colored pencils do not reproduce their tones with any degree of accuracy. I do much better using black pencils with which I can judge the shade of color I am trying for.

I use Grumbacher ink concentrate as I find that it has advantages over Artone (it is blacker and denser) and over Can-o-paque (the blackest and densest). Grumbacher ink washes off easily with soap and water, and I can make small corrections (Q-Tips rubbed on a bar of soap are useful for this). On the other hand, Can-o-paque washes off entirely too easily. It comes off at the slightest touch and will smear unless one's hands are kept completely off the work. Also, when corrections are necessary it is impossible to wash off a small area without washing off everything nearby. All these inks are very hard on brushes. Since it is fatal to let the ink dry on the bristles, I always keep a glass of water handy so that brushes are dunked immediately. They must be washed out daily with soap and water, too.

A danger with both inks is that even after they are dry they tend to reabsorb moisture from the atmosphere and get wet and tacky. We have a lot of foggy weather on the coast here in Maine, and I find that I have to store my finished work in a very dry room. As yet I haven't used a dehumidifier, but I may come to that. If the ink should get tacky and the Dinobase plates stick together, the work can be ruined. To be on the safe side I always place sheets of wax paper between each piece of finished work.

I like to bleed my backgrounds; and often when the background is all one color I do the plate in reverse: all the black ink comes out white on the colored blackground when printed. You can get some lovely, delicate lacy white patterns. I did the end papers for *The Wonderful Egg* this way; and in *Brown Cow Farm* I did almost all the backgrounds in reverse. The spread with the rabbits is a good example, with its delicate white flowers and foliage outlined against chartreuse.

Visitors look at my light table and separations all set up and are shocked that in this day of photographic reproduction processes the artist still has to make each color plate himself. In a way it *is* ironic. The machine was once a cheap substitute for human labor; now human labor is infinitely cheaper than the machine (reproduction by camera four-color process is fabulously expensive!).

But although it looks like tedious labor, I enjoy doing separations. It is in these Dinobase or wash drawings that the final decisions as to tone and line and composition are made and carried through. And it is always exciting to see the first proofs, combining all the separate plates at last into a finished work of art.

From *The Horn Book Magazine*, February 1966.

The colophon designed by Lynd Ward to signify "The Artist at Work" series has been used as the jacket drawing for this volume.

DOING A BOOK IN LITHOGRAPHY
by Lynd Ward

. . . Where Doré or Cruikshank were boxed in with only two or three ways of making a drawing that could be printed on a book page, today's reproductive processes have opened the door to literally everything — from the lush, rough solids of a woodcut to the delicate tracery of the most gossamer pen line; from the flat grays of a poster technique to the subtlest of graduated washes; from a controlled use of two or three simple colors to the unbelievable complexity of a painting in full color.

There has, of course, been a price to pay for all these riches. And that price has been in departmentalization. Increasingly the artist is separated from the craft steps whereby the image he has created is actually impressed on the paper. . . . [T]he artist [is] involved, not in the whole process, but in the first step only.

It is, I think, giving away no secrets to say that this separation from the whole process can be a source of frustration. Despite . . . technical virtuosity . . . the printed page today sometimes turns out to be less than a complete realization of what the artist intended. Where so many other hands are involved in the process, it is easy for an artist to feel, when he compares the printed page with his original, that "someone else" is to blame. There are, happily, certain ways of working that involve the artist more completely than others, and of these none allows — or requires — quite as much involvement as does working in lithography.[1] This is the old method of drawing directly on stone that in another century served Daumier and Toulouse-Lautrec so well, and in this country provided the basis for the unique operation carried on by Currier and Ives. It is an old-fashioned way of working that has been harnessed to modern offset

1 "Lithography" is a term which has come to be synonymous with "photo-offset," a widely used method of printing. The process Mr. Ward describes involves the word in its original, literal meaning — "writing on stone."

87. Illustration by Lynd Ward for *The American Indian Story* by May McNeer, Farrar, 1963, 7¾ x 10½.

printing. It by-passes the camera completely and involves none of the photo-reproductive light-sensitive techniques that underlie most other ways of producing printed pictures. It requires its own materials, presses, and craftsmen: above all, craftsmen with a special body of knowledge, a special body of experience, and a special sensitivity to the capacities of the medium and the goals of the artist. . . .

George Miller occupies a unique place in the world of printing and in the world of art, too. Coming from a family with lithographers on both sides for several generations back, he has printed the stones of such old masters as Albert Sterner and George Bellows, has worked for years with men like Rockwell Kent, Stow Wegenroth, and Adolf Dehn, and has taught the rudiments of lithography to more artists than he — or anyone else — can remember. His son Burr has worked with him for fifteen years now, and together they make a team that handles with unequalled competence every aspect of their craft.

When I start a book that is to be done in lithography, such as *The American Indian Story*, the first step, after completing rough sketches for all the pictures that are to be in the book, is to stop in for a talk with the Millers. On the basis of my sketches, we work out an estimate of the number of stones that will be required and set up a tentative schedule for completion of the drawings, proving the stones, transferring, plate-making, and finally the actual press run. The final point on which we agree is the time for me to pick up the stones.

This last is a bit more complicated than it sounds, for on the day in question I come in from New Jersey in the station wagon. . . . [I]f I have estimated my travel time correctly, the Millers' shop assistant, Dave, has just arrived on the sidewalk with a pile of lithographic stones on a dolly.

The stones are flat slabs of limestone, usually measuring sixteen by twenty inches and about three inches or so thick. They vary in weight from fifty to eighty pounds and . . . have all been carefully ground down with powdered carborundum to a smooth clean surface on both sides, then given a beautiful fine grain with a finer carborundum. Each one is wrapped in clean white paper, for the whole process of lithography hinges on the sensitivity of the stone to anything that touches it. The protection of its surface is of primary concern at every step of the way.

In the studio, one of the stones is blocked up on the drawing table with a piece of wood under its far edge to keep the under surface, which will also be drawn on, from touching. Every artist has his own way of working, but for me the first step is a fairly careful tracing of the rough sketch. The back of the tracing paper is rubbed with brown pastel or sanguine conte crayon, which means that the traced lines appear on the surface of the stone in brown lines that give a clear guide to the composition of the drawing but give it in a chalklike material that is completely neutral and has no effect on the sensitivity of the stone. Some artists may prefer to attack the stone directly with no preliminary sketch. There are, however, two points to be remembered. First, the drawing on the stone must be the exact dimensions of the area it is to occupy on the finished page of the book; second, although minor corrections can be effected after the crayon is applied to the stone, major changes, or the kind of obliteration and complete reworking that many other media allow, are just not possible.

With the drawing laid out on the stone in the traced lines, the work with crayon begins. For those who have once got the taste of it, there is nothing quite like working on stone. The artist has a limited range of tools to employ: crayon in varying degrees of hardness in two forms, either short square sticks or spiral-wrapped pencils; rubbing ink, which allows a delicate tone to be rubbed on an area of the stone with the ends of the fingers wrapped in cloth; touche, which is ink in stick form to be rubbed onto a saucer, then diluted with water and applied to the stone either with a pen or more freely with a brush. Regardless of which of these drawing materials is used, the essential point is that each is a compound of grease, wax, and lampblack, whose function is to apply grease in varying amounts to certain areas of the stone. The black of the crayon is in effect a visualizing agent whose presence in the substance with which the artist works enables him to gauge the amount of grease that is going onto the stone — and where. It is the presence of the grease, not the black, the enables the stone to produce a printed image.

111

Working with one of these materials or with all of them in combination, the artist gradually develops the subject on the stone. The first strokes of the crayon, if applied lightly, will give a delicate line, or, if extended carefully over an area, will lay down a medium tone that can be worked over gradually with a rotating stroke to bring up an ever-darkening gray. Rich blacks can be brushed in with the liquid touche, or built up a bit at a time by using softer crayon over a layer of harder crayon. Pure whites — either in large areas, small flecks, or fine line — can ultimately be added by scraping with a razor blade. But this scraping must be done with care, since an area once scraped loses its surface grain and will not therefore allow any redrawing that seeks the same grained crayon stroke that the original surface of the stone produced so beautifully. While drawing, the artist must keep his hands from touching the stone by resting them when necessary on a folded rough towel or on a wooden bridge that arches slightly and thus keeps the undrawn surface of the stone free from accidental blemishes. A thumbprint, invisible to the eye, will contain enough grease from the skin to come up in the printing; a sneeze or a cough that catches the stone full in the face can be equally disastrous.

When several stones have been filled on both sides with drawings, they travel back to the city to meet Dave on the sidewalk again, then go upstairs to the shop. There they undergo the first of several administrations of a chemical nature that bring them to the point of proofing. Through the cooperative actions of gum arabic, mild acids, asphaltum, rosin, and several other substances that do the bidding of magicians and skilled lithographers like George and Burr Miller, the surface of the stone becomes intricately separated into two mutually antagonistic areas; the parts that have been drawn on are grease-sensitive, the undrawn parts are water-sensitive. When the stone is dampened with water and rolled up with a leather roller charged with greasy ink, the drawn areas receive the ink and the undrawn areas repel it. Then, when a dampened sheet of paper is laid on the stone and the whole pulled through a hand press in which a scraping pressure forces the paper onto the stone, the drawn image is transferred to the paper, and the artist sees for the first time what he has been working for through all the preliminary stages. At this point, it is possible to make minor corrections if in the proof something shows up that until now was unforeseen.

When all the drawings that are to go on a single press sheet have been proved up, the Millers undertake the next step. This is to pull proofs on a special transfer paper, a curious substance which has an ultrasensitive, gelatine-like coating. These transfer proofs are placed face down on a sensitized metal press plate, which already has had the type areas fixed on it photographically, and are run through a larger hand press. This step fastens the proof fast to the press plate; and when the backing of the transfer paper has been sponged off and the whole carefully etched, washed out and rolled up, the drawings that were originally on stone have been transferred without change or modification to a plate that can then be locked into an offset press that will print thousands of copies at high speed through the complicated magic of modern technology.

For those pages in the book that are to be done in color, the procedures are basically the same, but extended in scope. For color work, a fairly complete sketch is almost mandatory, for it must provide a guide not only for the various elements of the subject but must also indicate the amount, kind, and location of every color that is planned for the final picture.

Although in theory any number of colors can be used in printing a color lithograph, in actuality the economic factors require a limit, which most publishers usually set at three colors plus black. So, in working out sketches for the subjects that are to be rendered in color, it is essential that all the thinking and planning be done with a constant awareness of just what three inks will actually be mixed up and put into the fountain of the press when the sheets are finally printed. These basic colors are usually some variation of red, yellow, and blue, because the overprinting of any two of these will yield another intermediate hue. Thus, when the sketch is being worked out, the artist in effect has a palette in the back of his mind consisting of the three basic inks he will be working with, plus the additional colors that various combinations will produce. And when doing the black drawing on stone for what is to become a full-color project, the artist has to work from a sketch that is complete enough to tell him how much black tone he should put in a sky, for example, to produce the grayed blue that his sketch indicates will result from an overprinting of black on blue. Thus the black drawing on stone not only renders the basic subject in all its complexity of component parts, but also accords to those parts whatever varying amounts of black or gray are necessary to produce the modifications of other colors that his concept requires.

When the first stone with the black drawing of a full-color subject has been completed, it goes into the shop for the development of a trial color proof. This requires that after going through the same proving procedure that an ordinary black-and-white subject is accorded, wet proofs are dusted with brown chalk powder, which, when placed face down on fresh stones and run through the hand press, fixes on the new stones a replica of the black drawing in nonprintable brown. This affords a guide to the artist which enables him to draw, again with black crayon, on a second stone whatever elements in the subject are yellow, or have a

88. Illustration by Lynd Ward for *The American Indian Story* by May McNeer, Farrar, 1963.

percentage of yellow in them; on a third stone whatever elements are red or contain red; and on a fourth whatever elements are blue. These additional stones are then proved up in colored inks which have been carefully mixed in accordance with the special colors originally decided on. And when the four stones are carefully printed one after another on a single sheet of paper, the subject, which previously existed as four different parts, gradually takes shape; and for the first time the artist sees the color print towards which he and the Millers have been working all these weeks.

The purpose of this trial hand proof from stone is to enable the artist to see whether his first decisions about what precise colors to use and how they would combine in overprinting were the right decisions, for now he goes back to completing the black drawings for all the pages that are to be in color. When these are done, the Millers prove up the stones, make transfers to the press plates, and from these press plates make off-sets in brown chalk onto new plates, one for each color. Then, using the brown chalk as a guide, the artist draws the additional colors with black crayon, just as was done on stone for the trial stone proof.

When all these color plates are drawn, if you are the artist, the most hazardous and nerve-racking part of the operation begins. For some weeks the shop has been crammed with the terrifyingly huge skids of paper; the supplier has sent over enormous cans of ink compounded to match the color samples agreed upon; the press has been oiled, the fountain filled with an unbelievable dark molasses-like substance that George Miller assures you will roll out exactly like the yellow specified; the yellow press plate is micrometered and its backing sheets adjusted to the proper number of ten-thousandths of an inch. The switch is thrown and the press begins to roll.

The first sheets that come through are ill-printed and out of line; but adjustments are made, and after a while, a sheet comes through that is brought for inspection. You look at the four semi-abstract shapes scattered in checkerboard fashion over the sheet, and you try to remember just how much yellow was supposed to be in this one, how much in that one, and how strong or how light a tone. You suggest lightening one unit here, darkening one there; and because it is a small press and the

subjects occupy separate horizontal areas of the paper, it is possible to adjust the amount of ink that is fed onto the parts of the long rollers that ink each subject. Thus a drawing that is to have a strong yellow can be fed the right amount of ink to produce that yellow and conversely another drawing that needs only a faint kiss of color can have its ink supply cut down to produce it.

When the second color is put on the press and the first sheets come through, you can see not only how the strength of color should be adjusted but, if there are places where you have drawn the color a little outside the area in which it should be contained, Burr will stop the press and you can take a long sliver of abrasive stone, rub off the extraneous crayon marks, and bring the drawing back to what it should be. And so on through the addition of the other colors and the completion of the full four colors that were planned.

The involvement of the artist in this entire long process makes him a partner with the craftsmen who carry out the practical steps whereby the image drawn on the stone becomes the image that appears on the printed page. This, then, is a very special way of working, which avoids the frustrations inherent in the more modern procedures where the artist inevitably feels that "someone else is to blame." Here, of course, because he is so closely integrated with the development of his book from first step to last, there is no one to blame but himself for whatever is lacking in the result. But there is also the rare and saving circumstance that he can learn from what went wrong this time, and next time come just a bit closer to his goal.

Excerpts from the article which appeared in *The Horn Book Magazine*, February 1964.

SCRATCHBOARD ILLUSTRATION

by Barbara Cooney

... I often puzzle over the work of other illustrators, trying to figure out how they achieve their results. I pore over books on printing and on the graphic arts, but I cannot seem to find the answers in books. I ask questions at publishing houses and at printing plants. I try to see the original artwork of other illustrators ... I buttonhole other illustrators and ask them questions, although it seems like prying from chefs their secret recipes. Printing and illustrating techniques are developing constantly. New materials appear on the market. New ways are developed for using these materials. However, from what little I have learned, it seems that most illustrators are feeling their own way amid these new developments, evolving their own methods of work, fashioning their own tools. There seems to have been no common pool from which to fish the answers. Therefore, I welcome this series of articles on the artist at work because it promises to provide me with some of the answers for which I have been looking.

Though there is nothing very new or tricky about making a scratchboard illustration, I am happy to add my two cents to this series and to tell what I know about this particular technique, its advantages and disadvantages, the way I handle the medium, what materials I find best to use, and a few pitfalls to avoid.

Each illustrating medium has a character of its own. Like wood engraving, which it resembles in appearance, scratchboard has an affinity for the printed page. The crisp, forthright technique makes a happy marriage with the clean letters of type. The flat black-and-white surface of the drawing preserves the flat surface of the page and the unity of text and illustration. For the artist, the medium is a good disciplinarian. It allows no subterfuge, no sketchy representations, no incomplete

Barbara Cooney's early illustrations were often done in a scratchboard technique. Later, she used a black-and-white scratchboard as the key drawing and a Dinobase overlay for each color. This was the preseparated art technique she used for Chanticleer and the Fox, *awarded the 1959 Caldecott Medal.*

statements. Weaknesses cannot be hidden. The results may be delicate or brutal, but they are never indecisive. In short, the artist must know how to draw and he must draw with precision, for there is a finality too in drawing on scratchboard. Erasures and corrections are difficult and often impossible. The artist must think in terms of a limited palette, in bold black and white with perhaps five in-between grays, obtained by parallel lines, crosshatching, or stippling. These grays can be either black on white or white on black. When the plates are well made, the paper good, and the printing well done, the printed illustration is very close to the original drawing, a characteristic most gratifying to an illustrator.

Let us assume that a book has been designed, the galley proofs have been cut up, and the type pasted into a blank dummy. I generally attack the illustrations by starting methodically at the front of the book and working toward the back. From the dummy I know exactly how much space is required on each page for both text and illustration and where each is to go.

I begin by making a careful drawing on tracing paper. This is the exact size the illustration will be in the book because I like to have a fairly accurate idea of how the printed page will look. To my mind, too much is lost if the drawing is made larger than it will appear in the book and then reduced by the printer. There is always a loss between the drawing board and the book, anyhow.

Next, I transfer this drawing onto the scratchboard. To do this I rub with a pencil on the back side of the tracing-paper sketch, making a sort of home-made carbon paper. Then I place the tracing-paper sketch face up on the scratchboard, which is also face up, and by going over the drawing with a hard pencil transfer it to the scratchboard.

Scratchboard is a drawing board, one surface of which is coated with a smooth, white, chalklike surface, which takes ink readily. You can draw with black ink on the white surface and by scraping (scratchboard is called "scraperboard" in England) or scratching through a black-inked surface with a sharp instrument, you can draw in white on a black surface. I use Extra Heavy Ross Scratchboard. I find that the surface of the heaviest scratchboards are superior to the thinner sorts.

89. India ink applied with brush on scratchboard.

90. Finished art demonstrating how various textures
are scratched into the black drawing. Illustration
by Barbara Cooney for *Grandfather Whiskers, M.D.*
by Nellie M. Leonard, Crowell, 1953.

After transferring the sketch to the scratchboard, I
go over the drawing carefully with a pencil before
I ink it in, thus leaving little to chance or last-
minute inspirations –– or mistakes. Since pencil
lines on scratchboard are not always easy to erase, I
use a blue pencil. The blue lines will not be picked
up by the camera when the plates are made.

Now comes the inking in. I cannot overstress the
use of a really black ink for proper reproduction.
The camera must lose none of the areas that are
meant to be black. There are several good black
inks on the market. I myself use Artone Extra
Dense Black Ink. To put the ink on the scratchboard I use a pen from time to time for such things
as dotted areas, but generally I use a brush.

Brushes are preferable to pens because pens cut
into and trip on the chalky surface. Except for large
black areas, I use very small brushes. These are
invariably Winsor and Newton Series #7, red-
sable triple-zero brushes. I also have a few larger
brushes whose points I have cut off, which I use
for stippling. Because ink and paint left in brushes
overnight will shorten their lives and ruin them by
rotting the hairs, I will repeat here the old saw that
an artist's only morality is to keep his brushes
clean.

After the drawing has been wholly or partly
inked in, the scraping and scratching begin. For
crisp sharp lines the ink should be thoroughly dry.
So should the scratchboard surface, which tends to
hold moisture in humid weather when the win-

116

dows are open. A hand hairdryer is useful at these times, but it is better still to store the scratchboard supply in a closet equipped with a dehumidifier. I use various instruments for the scraping and scratching operation. I have tried various tools sold specifically for this purpose, but only two have been of any value to me. These are a small diamond-shaped blade and a small oval blade, both set in wooden handles. At one time I used a phonograph needle set in a holder. More practical has been a collection of dental probes, which I file down to sharp points. Recently I have found an X-acto knife with a #11 blade useful. One essential piece of equipment is a sharpening stone, which I use constantly. Another essential for me is a watchmaker's loupe for examining the cleanness and sharpness of my lines.

As for scratchboard illustrations printed in more than one color, this is my system for preseparated artwork: Only the black key plate is made on scratchboard. Each other color is drawn separately onto a transparent overlay. I use Dinobase for this purpose with Artone Extra Dense Black Ink. As for the scraping and scratching, the #11 X-acto blade is the tool I use. Dinobase does not have the easy-to-scratch surface of scratchboard, but the result, when printed, is a reasonable facsimile thereof.

Scratchboard, however, is primarily a black-and-white medium. The mastery of a crisp black-and-white technique is a useful string for any illustrator's bow. Editors want it because not only is it less expensive to print but it is so suited to the printed word.

Excerpts from the article which appeared in *The Horn Book Magazine*, April 1964.

THE CROW-QUILL PEN

by Ed Emberley

Although I have employed many different tools in preparing illustrations, the one I use most frequently is the crow-quill pen.

Of the pen points available, I prefer a Gillott

No. 659 crow-quill point in a Gillott black wood holder. The point is not standard in that it is small and the end that attaches to the holder is tubular instead of the more common half-round shape. The point slips over the end of the holder, which is dowel shaped. Although I use many kinds of ink, Higgins waterproof black is my most frequent choice. I prefer Strathmore one-ply drawing paper with a kid finish that has a little more tooth to the hot-pressed variety, which is as smooth as glass. The former is hard enough to keep the extremely sharp pen point from sticking into it, translucent enough to trace through with the aid of a light table, and tough enough to use an electric erasure on. An electric erasure serves me better than white paint for making corrections, since it is quicker and cleaner, leaving a surface that will accept a pen-and-ink line. White paint will not accept a pen-and-ink line; the surface is so soft and absorbent that the point digs in and the line blurs and blots. Large corrections are made by cutting out the area and substituting a new drawing.

Here are some of the things the pen can do: it can make lines which are thick, thin, or of varying thickness. It can make small solid areas. (Large solid areas are usually made with a brush.) It can create various shades of gray with parallel lines or crosshatching. It can, if a colored ink is used, create by means of crosshatching various shades of the color from light to dark. It can, by crosshatching one color over another, produce a third color. For example, blue crosshatching over yellow will make green.

A good example of the crow-quill pen at work is the accompanying illustration from *Punch and Judy*. My inspiration for doing this book came from studying a set of etchings by George Cruikshank for the first American edition of the Punch and

---

Ed Emberley has a Master of Fine Arts degree from Massachusetts College of Art and attended Rhode Island School of Design. He worked in advertising before writing and illustrating children's books. He likes to use his own small handpress to experiment with type and woodcuts, often pre-printing the artwork he then hands to the printer. In 1968 his illustrations for Drummer Hoff *won him the Caldecott Medal. In recent years he has done many books in pen and ink.*

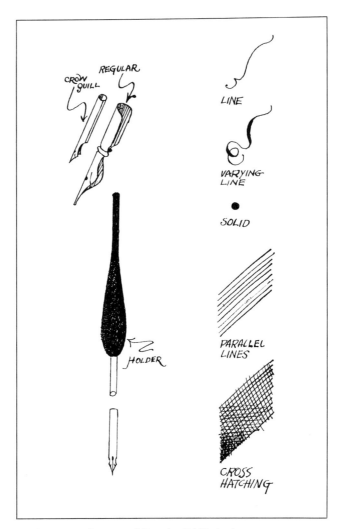

91. Diagrams of pens and lines by Ed Emberley.

Judy play, which I found in the Harvard University Library. In modeling my Punch after Cruikshank's marvelous Mr. Punch, it was natural for me to make the sketches with the crow-quill pen, for its effects are similar to those created by the etching needle. Having used the pen for the sketches it was natural for me to use it for the book itself.

In the finished printed book, the spot shown is in solid magenta, yellow, and blue. By using lines, crosshatching, and solid areas in various combinations, I gained three "free" colors: green (blue crosshatching printed over solid yellow); vermillion (magenta crosshatching over solid yellow); and purple (magenta crosshatching over blue crosshatching).

In the finished printed book, the spot shown was in solid color as follows: the Devil, all magenta; the Hangman, green face, dark green cheeks, darker green costume; and Mr. Punch, pink face, vermillion costume with yellow trim.

The illustrations show the four drawings necessary to accomplish this effect. A black-line drawing for each color must be made. From these the printer makes plates — for each color — which, in combination, print the complete illustration as the artist originally visualized it.

The crow-quill pen is a sensitive, versatile tool, one of my good and faithful friends.

From *The Horn Book Magazine*, October 1966.

92. Drawings by Ed Emberley for *Punch and Judy, A Play for Puppets,* Little, Brown, 1965.

119

SOME PROBLEMS OF A WRITER-ILLUSTRATOR

by Edwin Tunis

The numbers of writers who also draw, or of illustrators who also write, has increased lately. Probably the second combination, which applies here, is the more frequent. Illustrators have always cast covetous eyes at those royalties.

When illustrations are to be more than allusive, when they are integral with the text and serve to clarify description, the marshaling of words and drawings must in some measure proceed together. This creates special problems, which each person solves according to his lights and limitations. Perhaps the ideal writer-illustrator for my books would be a thoroughly grounded scholar who can draw. This is not impossible, but there is a catch in it. The scholar often becomes so scholarly, and so chary of other scholars' criticism, that he can no longer write the plain words that most of us like to read.

Since my problems begin with research, it is best to start there. The first question usually asked is, "Do you, or does your publisher, select your subjects?" (Perhaps "suggest" is a better word.) The answer is, nearly fifty-fifty, with a slight edge to the author. "How do you do your research?" HA! You find out from any possible source all you can about the subject. If there is a generalized book about it, you are way ahead. Such a book will provide a panorama, even if it turns out to be not quite accurate. Then, if one does not know enough, he must learn enough to understand what the real students have said about the matter. Libraries and librarians are involved, of course. It would be hard to overpraise either.

This small book factory is happily located near three great libraries and several excellent special-

Edwin Tunis is another artist-craftsman who came to the field of children's books in a roundabout manner, beginning as a furniture designer and then doing advertising artwork. Researching and painting a mural for a steamship company led to his book Cars, Sails and Steam, *one of the American Institute of Graphic Arts "Fifty Books of the Year" in 1953.* Frontier Living *was a Newbery Honor Book in 1962.*

ized ones, as well as five fine museums. When the quest leads farther, it has to be followed. Sometimes, as when I was studying the working methods of early American craftsmen, information must be dug out in bits and pieces. In that particular case it was checked as carefully as possible against foreign sources and by discussion with practising craftsmen. One can be flooded with information, too. It took help from the Smithsonian and some months of study merely to learn how to classify the mass of material that exists about American Indians.

A collection of file cards, sketches (made in museums or from book illustrations), and "scrap" is built up. As soon as an outline is possible, its headings serve as indicants for filing the lot into three files with identical indexes. Then comes the tough business of writing. In short spurts it goes well, but more often expanded outlines of each heading are needed. Then sudden holes appear which have to be filled. How was a sergeant's rank indicated in the Continental Army? A two-hour visit to the library reveals that he wore, on his right shoulder, one red epaulet, usually a strip of cloth, frayed at one end.

With a draft of the text completed, the what and how of the illustrations must be settled. A rough dummy of the whole book is needed. Illustrations must be numbered in order. The type space in the dummy is allotted by dead reckoning, and illustrations are indicated with crude sketches. By the time the last sketch is finished, the poor dummy is a wreck. It has erasures on every page; failures are covered with pasted paper; completely spoiled sheets are replaced and savable sketches from the removed sheets are pasted on the replacements. Normally such a dummy would be made up with galley proof, but that would be too costly here. Most of the galley would have to be reset. As each illustration is finished (perhaps in quite a different form than was indicated in the sketch) the description that it clarifies may have to be rewritten. The text may say too little, but it usually says too much. The weak spot in this system is the burden it places on the typographic designer. He must try to carry out the intent of the dummy, but he is hampered by the fact that the type space, even if it was nearly right in the first place, has now been made all

93. Illustration by Edwin Tunis for *Colonial Craftsmen and the Beginnings of American Industry* written and illustrated by Edwin Tunis, World, 1965.

wrong by the changes in text. I have reason to be grateful to several patient designers who have managed to keep words and illustrations within sight of one another without messing up pages.

Illustrations should be as pleasing as the illustrator's abilities permit, but their prime purpose in my books is clear explanation. They must try (they are never entirely successful) to put the object itself on the page. Drawings seem to come nearer to this than photographs usually can. Photographs have to be made with light, and light casts shadows, and shadows, though they make objects "stand out," also hide details. A drawing can force things a little and overcome the shadows.

I made pen drawings for the rather profuse illustrations of six books. Then, just as the quality of the work began to show signs of improvement, the "tight" drawing damaged a shoulder. As a result,

Colonial Craftsmen has crayon drawings, and the large ones for *Shaw's Fortune* are made with carbon pencils over light gray washes to "hold them together."

Erasures disturb the surface of a paper; a pen line drawn over an erasure sprouts feathers on both sides. The rather laborious system evolved to cope with this (which I still use) may have some interest. The drawing is roughed out with a soft pencil on tracing paper, and the struggle for composition, proportion, and action is fought out there. The paper is then turned over, and a cleaned-up outline is drawn on its back with a harder pencil. This is a mirror image, of course, but it comes right when it is placed face down on the drawing paper and is transferred by rubbing the soft-pencil side with a steel burnisher. The result is a light outline on a pristine surface.

From *The Horn Book Magazine*, December 1966.

94. Illustration by Edwin Tunis for *Frontier Living* written and illustrated by Edwin Tunis, World, 1961.

IV

Notes About Illustration
as Communication

The Book Artist and the Twenty-five Years

by Lynd Ward

... Essentially, this means that for the book artist the book as a whole is his medium of expression, and where earlier generations usually used a literary work as the jumping-off place for a drawing or a series of drawings thought of as having a more or less independent existence, now the individual drawing is only a single unit in the total picture, and a concern with the cumulative effect of all pictures plus all words is the essence of the book art.

This sharpened concept of the book artist's fundamental problem involved a greater emphasis on art as communication. Curiously enough, this took place at a time when the field of painting gave rise to overriding tendencies towards abstract and esoteric expression. The easel painter has become increasingly uncommunicative in his art, and where it was once possible for a man like Winslow Homer to be equally at home in a magazine, in a book, or when working on an independent canvas or watercolor, today a gulf increasingly separates the workers in these forms. As a major painter has expressed it, he is striving for an art that will exist completely independent of any other experience, so that the sensations or emotions that are evoked from seeing his work are entirely unrelated to any other sensation or experience. The book artist, on the other hand, must of necessity seek an art form that will integrate experience, not isolate it, will function in terms of the recognizable, and will build on the basic human tendency to associate experiences one with another, because from such cumulative associations come emotion and understanding.

It may seem paradoxical that two forms of visual expression should move in such divergent directions during the same span of years. And yet that very antithesis of goal has served to sharpen the book artist's definitions and has clarified his function in a way that nothing else could. It may very well be that what we see here is the separation of two elements that have always been present in the visual arts — the concern with communication and the concern with formal qualities that just "are," and are their own justification for being. In the minds of many, those two elements were always at war in painting, and from their point of view the present trend towards concern with formal qualities is inevitable and desirable. On the other hand, it can be contended that a balance between formal qualities in visual expression and concern with having something to say has resulted in some of the greatest visual statements of the past — Hogarth, Blake, Daumier, Goya, Callot, to name a handful — and that the ignoring of that long and meaningful tradition lay at the heart of the frustrations and maladjustments from which book artists have so recently matured.

... But the book artist has the feeling of being in working relation to an audience that is literally nationwide. It is a solid, honest relationship, for there is no medicine to be sold, and the emphasis is on straightforward communication from one person to another. There are no pressures, psychological or otherwise, to make things special or esoteric or of an increasingly narrowing appeal. ...

The twenty-fifth anniversary issue of The Horn Book Magazine, *September-October 1949, was devoted to a discussion of "Children's Books in Today's World," in recognition of books as an important element in communication. The excerpts here are taken from an article in which Lynd Ward described the maturing of the illustrator during that twenty-five-year period.*

Excerpts from the article which appeared in *The Horn Book Magazine*, September-October 1949.

Picture Books

by Joseph Low

The thing which is missing from most children's books is the thing which is at its peak in children's own work: spontaneous invention, emotional intensity, a natural use of the visual language. Why is it missing and how can it be recovered?

This quality, this freedom, this wonderful ability to create, is one of the most precious things children have, and as things stand, it is inevitably smothered out of existence or so hampered and twisted as they grow older that it might as well be nonexistent.

Children's great advantage in the beginning is that they are not yet self-conscious. No locks, no barriers, no fences prevent a free flow of invention and imagination. They just pick up a brush or crayon and go to work, scribbling and splashing about with the greatest freedom. Ideas pour out as fast as they can put them down. And the ideas find expression in the most natural way. They speak the visual language with no need for instruction from anyone. The best anyone can do is give them paint and paper; then step aside. The result may lack what we think of as technical finish, but it has a quality no mere professional skill can duplicate or replace.

Anything which helps to keep this quality alive in children is good. Anything which hinders it is

---

Joseph Low, who has illustrated a number of books for children, has taught design and graphic art at Indiana University; has often printed his own material on his Eden Hill Press. He has received awards from the American Institute of Graphic Arts. His prints and drawings have been acquired by various museums, libraries and private collectors; and he has received awards from the American Institute of Graphic Arts as well as other professional groups.

bad. And this applies to the illustrations in the books we give them. Too much of what they get now is pallid and lifeless or archly cute and sentimental. We need to do all we can . . . to put before them work which matches theirs in imagination and vitality, which does not imitate it in mannerism, certainly, but matches it in kind and goes beyond it in range and clarity.

The greatest problem which any artist faces in illustrating a book . . . is how to keep it fresh and alive in spite of the mechanical and human limitations which are imposed upon him. . . . How can he retain, through all the long process of roughs, layouts, fitting, finishes, separations, the freshness and unity and vigor which, if he succeeds, makes the completed work look as if it had been done easily, casually, delightfully, spontaneously?

By no means does the artist always solve that problem. Often he will find himself looking back at his first rough sketches, wishing he might recover the loose and easy quality they had. . . . It is the most valuable thing he has to offer and the hardest to maintain. It comes most easily when he is at ease, when he feels no pressure, when the gates are open and everything flows out, when there are no barriers to his imagination.

Anyone who has had a chance to see the work that an artist produces under these circumstances will know what I mean . . . the free roughs done before he begins "serious" work on a job, the things he tacks on his own wall to remind him of what he would like to get into *all* his work. . . . They have a freshness and ease which is not always present in his "finished" work.

The word finished always has a deadly sound in my ear. Too often it suggests finished like a neatly, tastefully, skillfully embalmed corpse lying in a coffin. Superficially, the body resembles a living creature, but clearly missing is whatever it was that made the man alive. And *that* is what makes the difference between a really excellent book and one which is no more than professionally competent, not to mention the hundreds which are not even that. The difference is elusive, delicate, easily damaged, but it is precious and vital.

It is what we must preserve and transmit to our children if we want them to grow and flourish. To the extent that the artist is alive when he is at work, the book will be alive. To the extent that the book is alive, it can bring life, freedom, and growth to the child who sees it. A child begins life with a wonderfully rich and free imagination. In the course of his education, both in and out of school, it is suppressed.

As he becomes self-conscious, he begins to feel society's pressure for conformity, for factual accuracy, for technical skill. He feels he must put aside his imagination and become a realist, a term of highest praise among the solid citizens who demand that he must "see things as they are," observe accurately and record minutely. In short, though born an artist, he must become a stock clerk taking inventory. He is made to look only out, never in, to record what he sees, not what he feels, because he lives in a society strongly dominated by a commercial middle class.

. . . Some survival of the old concepts and imagination persisted in folk art, but these were driven so far underground and regarded with such contempt by society in general and the aestheticians in particular that appreciation of them has only recently begun to re-form. I certainly do not want to encourage the production of any pseudo folk art. Nothing could be worse. True folk art can emerge only from a condition which does not and cannot exist in our society. Any attempt to revive it is bound to end in sentiment and bathos, in tricks and mannerisms, in yearning for a never-never land. True folk art is hard and tough and vital. Its imitation is soft and sweet or clever and cute, but it can never match the intensity of the real thing.

How can we recover and preserve for our children their natural heritage? We need a liberating art, one which frees and strengthens a child by encouraging him to use his own imagination, to keep it alive, perceptive, and growing. Too much of what he gets now works, consciously or not, to push him into a world of narrow respectability and trivial sentiment. Instead of feeding his powers, we starve them; instead of exercising, we stifle them. Is it any wonder that scarcely any survive who still retain the gift? . . .

Ideally, a good picture book should look as if it had been done on the spur of the moment, at one sitting, especially for the child who is looking at it; it should be done by someone with a fresh idea, the ability to express it graphically, and a strong wish to give it to another.

The best possible circumstance would be one in which the artist-author (ideally the two roles are combined in one person) works for a small group of children whom he knows intimately so that a strong stimulus may pass back and forth between them, both sides taking and giving, to build the pictures and the story and give them life.

There would be no limitations of size, of printing processes, of market considerations, of layout. The thing would begin, grow, and reach its fruition unrestrained, free to expand, if that seemed good, or to remain small, distilled, if that seemed better. While it is impossible to match this lovely condition in the actuality of publishing, something approaching it can be achieved by a sympathetic editor — one who draws from an artist the best that is in him. Unfortunately, the process by which picture books, like other books, are made is exceedingly cumbersome and places many restraints upon the artist and many blocks in his path, not because editors and publishers will it, but because of the ponderous mechanism of commercial production and distribution. The system requires elaborate and protracted organization and the cooperation of many people. It imposes dozens of technical problems, which, if the artist is not skillful, perceptive, and persistent, will defeat him and diminish his work. Whatever his potential may have been, he will have delivered only a small part of it. He must be both sensitive enough to conceive and tough enough to sustain his work if it is finally to reach the child for whom he intended it. . . .

Excerpts from the article which appeared in *The Horn Book Magazine*, December 1967.

95. Illustration by Joseph Low for *There Was a Wise Crow* written and illustrated by Joseph Low, Follett, 1969.

96. Illustration by Bettina for *The Magic Christmas Tree* by Lee Kingman. (This illustration was reproduced from the British edition, Oxford, 1957, for which the artist's original watercolors were used. The American edition, Farrar, 1956, was done by preseparated art.)

Story and Picture in Children's Books

by Bettina Ehrlich

. . . One day, shortly after my first children's book had been published, an artist friend of ours came to see us. Naturally I could not refrain from showing him my book. Looking at the pictures quickly but intensively, he said, "They're all right. Children will be able to read them well. Because, as you probably know, children *read* pictures — like this." And producing a babyish and friendly grunt he began to dab his forefinger on the various little details of one picture, as a person who reads might follow the printed lines with his finger, thus rendering a perfect imitation of a small child with a book.

What he had so exquisitely expressed I had, up to that time, only felt vaguely and instinctively.

I had, however, in previous years made a rather thorough study of children's paintings, had watched their creation and discussed them with the children. I had learned then that the child's painting is a *picture writing* and that it grows from

---

Bettina, as she signs her books, was born in Vienna, and attended schools there, but spent many months of her childhood on the island of Grado in the Adriatic Sea. She became a painter and graphic artist, hand-printing books and textiles. In 1938 she married, settled in London, and began writing and illustrating children's books, many of which have been published both in England and the United States. She prefers to use pen and ink, or water-color, and has a unique quickly recognizable style — sympathetic to children but unsentimental and lively.

entirely different roots and motives than do the paintings of adults.

The truly visual perception develops at a fairly late stage in the child and this is precisely the stage at which, very often to the disappointment of the parents, the child will gradually or suddenly stop painting. It is roughly the age of ten or a little later. Anyway it is the time when the child begins to see things as they really appear to the human eye and when he can read and write without difficulty.

The first factor, the birth of visual perception, discourages artistic reproduction in the average child as being too difficult. The second, the ability to write and read, makes painting as a means of expression superfluous and illustrations as explanatory additions to the word no longer essential. Therefore, the book in which the illustration has a predominant part will be considered "babyish" by the child of over ten and though he may enjoy it, his dignity will forbid this enjoyment to become too manifest.

The small child paints and draws to express his thoughts and wishes and not from the desire to reproduce the visible world around him. He usually paints objects which he loves or wishes to possess. (Mum and Dad and little self before the house; an airplane, a horse, etc.) He will also draw without flinching objects he has never seen, a thing the adult artist hardly dares to attempt, unless he takes refuge in the uncontrollable shapes of non-objective art.

The child combines in his paintings shapes he has seen and can remember and others which he freely invents (these, too, however, representing objects!) without being aware of any difference between the two and with inimitable ease and power of composition. Hence, the great charm of children's paintings. To the child himself, however, this charm is non-existent and only a very few children cherish their own paintings for more than a few days. If a child shows a tendency to preserve them, this, more than the quality of the paintings, might be taken as a sign of artistic disposition.

Furthermore, and this is important, the child cannot read, nor does he want to read other children's "picture writing," i.e., look at other children's pictures. For every child's picture writing is a secret

128

writing, understandable only to its creator and in need of explanations for everybody else. It is a writing made up, to a greater or lesser extent, of *personal symbols.*

Now, when we remember that as soon as a child can read lettering he wants clear, impersonal lettering — letterpress and not handwriting — we immediately understand that he will demand clarity also from the illustrations he has to *read*. Above all, they must be composed of universally valid symbols and not of personal ones such as those he uses himself.

This leads us quite naturally to see which are the most important qualities in illustrations for the young child.

The story told in the picture must correspond completely with the story told by words. If it is said in the story that a house stood near a forest, the forest must show up in the picture of the house. If a person in the story is described as wearing a green hat, green the hat in the picture must be. If green is denied to the illustrator by limitation of color imposed by economy or any other consideration, the only way out is for the author to change the text or for the illustrator to abandon the illustration of this particular passage. Incongruities of text and picture are unforgivable to the child and considered to be as absurd as it would seem to an adult to read, "His green hat was red."

On the other hand, a child will not usually mind a black and white drawing which illustrates a passage where color is mentioned. Imagination will fill the gap. But it is far better to avoid mentioning colors too much in a book which will be illustrated in black and white.

The importance of bright colors for children's book illustration is, I think, generally much overrated by the adult who buys the book and consequently by all those in the bookselling trade who cater to the child via the adult.

It is true that smaller children have a tendency to grab brightly colored objects, especially red ones. This, however, is really a consequence of their undeveloped faculty of visual discernment. Only a few children can distinguish subtle shades of one color or remember subtle colors. The defined and outspoken is easy to distinguish and red is the color that "strikes" the eye most.

However, when it comes to illustrations in a book, the contents of the picture, its "readability," and a certain quality which I should like to call "intimacy" or "lovability" are more important. The picture should offer a lot to read; it should, above all, go into detail. A picture which offers a few facts and which one has finished "reading" in a second is unsatisfying for the small child however great its artistic merits in design, composition and color may be.

It cannot be emphasized enough that the picture is not taken in as a whole any more than the type face of a page is taken in as a whole by the reading adult. The picture is *dissected* into its details, and the more meaning it conveys the better. I think this must be the explanation for the fact that children often adore pictures which, to the eye of the discriminating adult, show no beauty and no artistic achievement. . . .

Thus the picture for the child . . . should convey information, meaning, story, detail. In order to produce good as well as beautiful illustrations for children the artist must love children and understand their needs. He should also, to a certain extent, have a lively recollection of his own childhood, an ability to creep back into it and to recall what it felt like to be little. However, he should never try to paint like a child!

The imitation of children's art is a great danger in contemporary illustrations of the more sophisticated brand. Never can this method lead to a good result. The adult artist has neither the naïveté nor the imagination to produce the picture writing of the child, and to attempt it is as objectionable as it would be for an adult writer to express himself in baby language or to spell as a child does. No one would appreciate that. "Talking down" to children has fortunately been condemned. Yet "painting down" to them is not only endured but often encouraged . . . The child, like every unspoilt human being, wants perfection and not regression into artificial babyishness.

One word, I think, should also be said about a certain type of balloon-headed children and pets which crop up all too frequently in children's books. The desire to create lovable and cuddly creatures, especially little animals, is, I suppose, re-

I'll jump over pieces of sky in the gutter.

97. Illustration by Uri Shulevitz for *Rain Rain Rivers* written and illustrated by Uri Shulevitz, Farrar, 1969, 9⅞ x 9.

The water then began to flow in, accompanied by the fish and all the water animals.

sponsible for this fashion. But a drawing, however free and personal, based on the profound study of nature will, I believe, convey the lovable and the moving much better. The wrinkles on a puppy's forehead, the enormous beak of a baby chicken, are features that make us love them but I cannot see that the fact that a creature is hydrocephalic makes it particularly adorable.

Yet proportion, in a much more dramatic sense, means a lot to children because they are continually confronted with the problem of size in their daily life, being themselves small compared with their surroundings, their parents, older children, etc. Therefore the counterplay of big and small is an important factor in illustrations. . . . Because size also plays a big role in the child's possessiveness and natural greed, the elaboration of fascinating proportions in children's book illustrations may be of greater value than the use of bright colors.

If I now try to sum up what I believe to be most important in writing and illustrating for children I would say it is: to give them, apart from the obviously needed facts and information, a wide and manifold idea of the world, beauty and emotional wealth.

Excerpts from the article which appeared in *The Horn Book Magazine*, October 1952.

98. Illustration by Blair Lent for *Why the Sun and the Moon Live in the Sky* by Elphinstone Dayrell, Houghton Mifflin, 1968, 8⅞ x 9.

Within the Margins of a Picture Book

by Uri Shulevitz

Mary Agnes Taylor wrote "In Defense of the Wild Things" (The Horn Book Magazine, *December 1970) as a response to unfavorable comments about the 1964 Caldecott Medal Book by Maurice Sendak,* Where the Wild Things Are, *made by Dr. Bruno Bettelheim in "The Care and Feeding of Monsters" (*Ladies Home Journal, *March 1969). While the gist of Taylor's article revolves around psychological premises, she brings out a basic point often overlooked in the recent development of almost voluptuously overwhelming picture books: "The fairy tale was developed primarily as a verbal and aural experience for adults; the modern picture book is basically a visual experience deliberately designed to transcend the verbal limitations of the very young. Although an aural experience usually accompanies the picture book, the fact remains that the young child must depend more on what he sees than on what he reads or hears if he is to comprehend the full meaning of a picture story." Taylor goes on to quote Bettelheim as emphasizing " 'that what the three-, four- or five-year-old needs is a clear, definite message,' " and then she states that "the modern picture book is advantageous for the preschool child, overcoming pictorially both the thematic abstractions of fairy tales and the limitations of infant vocabulary by visually giving the child the 'clear, definite message' Bettelheim demands."*

How an illustrator conceives, sees, develops, and communicates that 'clear, definite message,' both for young (as he has done in Rain Rain Rivers*) and slightly older children (in* The Fool of the World and the Flying Ship*) is described by Uri Shulevitz in the following article.*

Uri Shulevitz was born in Warsaw and spent his childhood in Poland and France. He studied at the Art Institute in Tel Aviv, did military service in Israel, lived in a kibbutz, was art director for a children's magazine, and found in children's books the perfect medium for his imagination and talent. For some years now he has lived and worked in the United States. His illustrations for The Fool of the World and the Flying Ship *retold by Arthur Ransome won the Caldecott Medal in 1969.*

After a story hour during which she had read *The Fool of the World and the Flying Ship: A Russian Tale* to a group of thirty-five black children, M. Isabel Mansfield, children's librarian of the Cleveland Public Library, wrote to my publisher:

One little boy who hitherto had displayed a very poor memory and little progress in reading in his first-grade class stood by one desk. As he turned the pages he told the story to another staff member in exact sequence using some of the complicated words. He was so moved that he wanted to keep the book. As the youngest of three brothers he felt akin to the young hero, and goes about calling himself the Fool of the World. The entire staff marveled at the power the book had on both a group of children and one individual boy — who for one brief moment displayed a latent ability to comprehend, follow, and even memorize a very complicated plot on a first hearing. . . . This is one of those rare moments which I as a children's librarian and dedicated story teller will cherish.

Despite the cultural remoteness of the tale, the little boy was deeply moved. The story reached him. He opened up, his intellectual capacities increased, and his potential was revealed. A small miracle had taken place. All as the result of a piece of fiction, a fantasy, a something-that-isn't-there. It is amazing, indeed, that something-that-isn't-there can have such an effect on something-that-is-there, that something fantastical can reveal and uncover something intangible. Images and pictures, those visible ghosts; words and ideas, those invisible sounds — can be potent indeed.

The Fool of the World and the Flying Ship is basically a traditional folk tale, its themes similar to those of other folk tales. We are so used to reading these stories automatically that we do not find anything unusual in them. We only see the usual wonders to be found in wonder tales of this kind. Thus, we tend to miss the story within the story, the inner substance, the life and energy that can engender the "small miracle."

The Fool of the World . . . begins by giving us a picture of the Fool's confinement at home, his prison — the symbolic walls which are made up of his mother's words: " 'Stupid fellow,' " she says, " 'What's the good of your going? Why, if you were to stir from the house you would walk into the arms of a bear; and if not that, then the wolves would eat you before you had finished staring at them' " — words probably repeated morning and night like an incantation. These walls become the very substance of the magic circle, out of which he must not step. Luckily, our Fool is foolish enough not to listen to his mother, otherwise he would still be lying on top of the warm stove, proving how right mother was. There would have been no new discoveries for him nor a tale for us to enjoy, and the princess would possibly still be single. Such walls are the hardest to break through, because they can be neither seen nor touched. But the Fool refuses to be bound by the ideas imposed on him and sets out to find a new world. The contrast between 'don't leave your warm place on top of the stove' and the flying ship sweeping freely through a boundless crystal-clear sky is no doubt exhilarating, both to our protagonist and to the reader. The story ends with the affirmation, that freedom is reachable despite all obstacles. The Fool finally succeeds and even enjoys the ride in the process.

Unfortunately, more often than one thinks, children are in a predicament at home similar to that of the Fool of the World. They feel hopelessly trapped, discouraged, misunderstood. Worst of all, most of the time they do not know the real reason for their misery. They are too weak to break through their prison walls. They are very vulnerable and can be easily crushed. Sometimes they play the Fool to survive. But most of them never get to marry the Czar's daughter. Instinctively knowing the danger, they eagerly seek sustenance to support their drive for life. They look for a refuge of security where they can grow and become stronger until they can stand on their own.

A picture book is not a silly little plaything. It is much more. Sometimes it can be everything to a child. A picture book can be a messenger of hope from the outside world. Its message, written in coded language, reaches the child in his prison, is understood by him while often hidden from the adult or the parent who is unwilling to listen to its true content or is simply insensitive to it.

It seems to me that in order to tune in on the wavelength that will penetrate prison walls and reach the child, all one has to do is tune in to a life-affirming attitude. Children are very sensitive to this, because their lives depend upon it. A destructive, life-negating attitude will not do. Neither will a saccharine approach. A picture book does not have to be deep, but it does have to be alive — whether it offers pleasure, joy, or sadness. I believe this point of view is essential to anyone interested in the field.

I first had the idea for my own picture book *Rain Rain Rivers* about five years before actually starting on the illustrations; it came and imposed itself on me in an unmistakable way. One evening I heard the patter of rain and simultaneously saw a series of images — impressions of which I immediately wrote down. This was the beginning. I thought that it was raining outside, since I could actually hear it. But when I looked out of the window, there was a clear night sky over the Greenwich Village rooftops. All this happened in a flash, and it was the seed of the future book. Subsequent work on the book — the unfolding, developing, extending, and organizing of the material — took considerably more time and effort. But everything was potentially there in the initial vision. The life substance of what was to come was there, provided I kept it alive by thought and care. As I worked on the pictures and the book gradually took shape, I began to distinguish in it the existence of different levels. In addition to the rhythm of rain, I felt in it the rhythmic beat of breathing. And so accordingly, I made the pictures large and small, small and large, as if breathing in and out; the energy accumulating, building to the final climax, and giving birth to splashes of joy. Colors in a rainbow, birds in the streets, children stamping in mud, the sky reflected in street puddles — a union of sky and earth through rain. When I reached the cli-

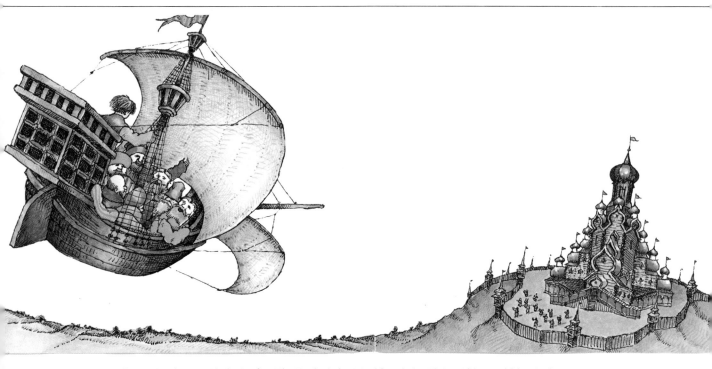

99. Illustration by Uri Shulevitz for *The Fool of the World and the Flying Ship* retold by Arthur Ransome, Farrar, 1968, 10⅜ x 9.

100. Illustration by Gerald McDermott for *Arrow to the Sun A Pueblo Indian Tale* adapted and illustrated by Gerald McDermott, Viking, 1974, 10⅝ x 9½.

The people celebrated his return in the Dance of Life.

mactic doublespread of the ocean, I felt like the ancient Greek philosopher who said: 'Everything is water,' meaning that everything in the universe consists of that substance in different states of consistency. In the ocean picture everything was brought back to its primordial state. As work was progressing, I felt that the little girl was making contact through the growth of the plant on the window sill of her room with the whole process of growth in the universe, and that in each drop of rain was contained a potential ocean, and in the child a potential of unlimited growth, energy, and freedom. All this had a definite purpose: to express what is real, to give hope, and to reinforce what is positive.

Unless we perceive and accept the fact that everything is related in a greater or lesser degree, nothing makes much sense and we are impoverishing our own resources. When I start on a new book, I try to see the images contained in the words of the story and to "listen" to the different pictorial elements and their impact, their orchestration, and whether they are expressing what I want them to. Although my natural way of thinking is through images, at some point there is a fusion of the different modes of expression. One "listens" with one's eyes, and "sees" through one's ears and fingers. For me, it is the small chaos preceding creation.

Ideas and thoughts make up our inner landscape and extend to what surrounds us. Life-affirming thoughts emanate energy that can stimulate the child to grow, expand, and even perform wonders. A picture book, like any other art form, has a life energy of its own. Take that away, and all you have left is an empty shell. Therefore, why not treat a picture book with care in order to make it grow — like a plant or an animal? One has to heed and nurture the something-that-is-there. Force it and it will die. For the process of artistic creation is an extension of the life process itself, and life itself is the supreme master.

From *The Horn Book Magazine*, June 1971.

How the Sun and the Moon Got Into a Film

by Blair Lent

Picture books are closer in spirit to motion pictures than to other kinds of books; and while working on many of my illustrations, I think about the visual movement from page to page, as well as about "long-shots" and "close-ups." When I begin to plan my pictures, I even use television storyboards (large pads of paper with squares for pictures and words), but the transition from a picture book to a film did not turn out to be a simple matter. My only previous experience with film had been ten years ago in an ad agency where I had drawn TV commercials for talking frankfurters.

Originally, I designed *Why the Sun and the Moon Live in the Sky* as if a pageant were being enacted by African tribesmen. Deliberately, I did not show heavenly bodies and natural phenomena; instead of actual water and sea creatures, I represented the water and the sea creatures as natives wearing masks. Since the main theme of the book is the long parade of Water and his people, I wanted the process to be very simple, taking place against a white background. The figures were always on the same scale, as though the book were a long stage. I had hoped that the film would embody these characteristics by presenting creatures of the same size throughout, small and toylike, and

The medium of film is continually becoming more important as the use of audio-visual materials in schools and libraries expands; film-making has become a popular subject in schools and colleges. Blair Lent's perceptions of how books and films about the same subject must differ in their creative process are particularly timely.

a parade moving against a solid-white ground.

After work started on the film, it became apparent that to repeat the book's presentation of the story would have been wrong, since in film it is often necessary to view faces and details closely. When a reader has a book in his hand, he can shift its position in order to examine details; and he can turn the pages as slowly or as quickly as he chooses. But in a film, the camera has to do what the reader's eyes do: it selects, dramatizes, and emphasizes. And the film itself is always going forward; but a picture book allows the reader to go back and forth at his own choice and pace.

With the assistance of Emily Jones, producer for ACI Films, and of Suzanne Bauman, the animator, the film *Why the Sun and the Moon Live in the Sky* was made in New York City. Before we met . . . I read several books on film animation and thought of a way of jointing cutout figures to make their arms, legs, and heads flexible. I even figured out a way of making the grasses on the African skirts rustle as the characters moved. . . . Suzanne later told me that she and Emily Jones had laughed about the moving grass. They explained to me that we would have to move a figure twenty-four times to make one second of film. Since the film was to be eleven minutes long, to do something as elaborate as moving blades of grass in the filming time we had at our disposal would have been next to impossible.

The next time I arrived in New York I came with a boxful of what I called cardboard puppets: cardboard figures with movable arms, legs, and heads — but no moving grass. . . .

We made the animated film on an apparatus called an animation stand. First, the artwork is arranged below the camera. Imagine a flat, jointed figure of a man. One frame (or more, depending on the effect wanted) is taken of him in a standing position. The camera stops; the animator reaches down and moves the figure's leg a fraction of an inch. Then, another frame is taken; the camera stops; and the figure's leg is moved a little more. The procedure continues until the figure has been moved through the desired actions. When the film is projected and the separate stills run by at the rate of twenty-four per second, the figure walks.

. . . Most commercial cartoons are made with what is called cel animation, in which a series of drawings are prepared on transparent acetate (Celluloid) by craftsmen. In this way one can produce smooth, almost lifelike, movements. But this was not the best method for *Why the Sun and the Moon Live in the Sky.* I wanted to be personally and closely involved with every aspect of the process and preferred not to have a group of people producing the animation. Also, I actually did not want the film to be smooth. Since it seems pointless to me for an animated film to look like real life, I favor the nonrealistic effect produced by the puppets.

A friend of Emily Jones's owned a small film studio, which was available for a month. . . . This studio's animation stand . . . had been constructed from many unrelated parts of camera equipment by one of the early experimenters with animated film. . . . Actually, Suzanne did most of the animating while I sat at the table nearby making new moveable characters and scenery. The delicate process of cutting around the edges of the artwork (many of the figures were only two inches high) and around the joints of the arms, legs, and heads took time. Often, eight figures were needed to represent one character — small ones, large ones, front views, back views, and side views. . . .

Actually, many new characters appear in the parade that are not in the book, and I would often create a figure to move in a certain way — a figure with a cloak that would open, for example; or one that could leap or crawl or snap its jaws. Suzanne would then take the figure and "choreograph" it. . . . Sometimes, the movement of the figures suggested a new direction for the plot. Scenes that had not appeared in the book were created and filmed, and the main characters began to take on distinctly new personalities. Water emerged as a rather sinister, menacing creature. Some of these innovations I felt were good; yet I thought it would be wrong to get too far from the simplicity of the original. But the final decisions were saved for the editing.

The background of the book also required changes. A dominant white background creates a glare on the screen; a tinted or colored background is better. The film, therefore, begins with a light yellow ground, which turns to deeper yellow when Sun and Moon build their house, to light blue when the water creatures begin to arrive, to deep blue as the flow increases, and almost to black at the end. These effects were achieved by placing large sheets of colored paper behind the figures and the scenery. With special lighting, we gradually intensified the colors as the story developed. . . .

We would look forward eagerly to getting the rush proofs of our film from the processing company. . . . But it was always a little surprising and maddening to see a scene we had spent hours creating flash by in an instant. . . . However, when we finished shooting, we had thirty-five minutes of film, which was much more than we had planned to use . . . [but] it gave us a choice as to what to use in the finished film and made it possible for us to experiment with the editing.

The editing of a film is a fascinating process, just as important as the actual shooting. The original negatives are not touched, but a cheap workprint of the film is snipped into many small pieces. These pieces are spliced together in any desired order. Two pieces of film shot weeks apart, for instance, will frequently end up beside one another; pieces shot at the very beginning can appear at the end of the film; some scenes are cut in half; and others are inserted. And while the scenes are being arranged and rearranged, again and again — they are constantly being shortened and discarded. It is exciting, creative work, for at this time the mood, the plot, and the emotional impact of a film finally take shape. Simply by editing, many different stories can be told with the same film. . . .

During the editing, we made our final decisions as to how far we should depart from the original story; and some departures were necessary. I do not think that the filmed version of a story should correspond exactly with that of the book. Film is a different medium, and is most effective when telling a story in its own way. Furthermore, an eleven-minute film requires a greater articulation of subject matter than does a thirty-two-page book. But one must be careful. If certain additions are not sympathetic to the spirit of the original, the quality of the film can be spoiled. And if too much extraneous material is added, a simple story can become obscure and complicated.

The sequence in which Sun and Moon build their house provides a good example of film editing. In the book, the house building is shown as a single action on a two-page spread, but in the film the whole process is shown. . . . As we worked, one idea led to another. For example, when the house was finished, Moon planted two flowers by the door, flowers which *do* appear in the book, without any indication of how they got there. We also made use of time indications to show that the house building took more than one day. . . .

The film was finished in Cambridge a few weeks after I left New York. Suzanne arrived with a partially edited version. She also brought the taped narration. Spencer Shaw had made several recordings in New York, experimenting with different ways of telling the story. It was difficult to decide which version was the best; for in all of them, he had captured just the right spirit. But, at last, one was chosen to be added later to the sound track.

As for the music, a screen was set up beside a piano in my studio. A print of the film was projected over and over again while [William Sleator] composed on the piano. In another room, Suzanne set up her film editing equipment and began working on the final version. . . .

The film was finally cut to eleven minutes, and the music composed. Now Jim Ellis, who plays several percussion instruments, and Franklin Hammond, who plays the cello, arrived for a long day of rehearsals. Again, the film was projected over and over; my studio was filled with the sounds of the children of friends who dropped by. A pot of chili simmered on the stove. I have often felt that the work of an illustrator can be lonely. Film-making is certainly not.

The recording for the film was made at a studio in Revere, just outside of Boston. The film was projected from a sound booth to prevent the sound of the projector from being recorded. The screen was the largest on which we had so far viewed the film. The musicians, including Suzanne with tambourine and me with bells, gathered around the screen and watched the film as we performed the music. A synchronizing device was used in the sound booth to make sure that the music would match the film perfectly.

The music was recorded several times. Halfway through the final recording, Bill, Jim, and Frank began — as usual — to improvise. But this time, caught up by the spirit of the music, the mood of the film, and the tension of the studio, the musicians gave new life to their performance. This recording, better than any of the others, was chosen unanimously to be used on the film.

Back in New York the negative was cut and spliced by technicians to reproduce exactly the edited workprint. This part of the process is done by professionals because a mistake made in preparing the negative can never be corrected: Any scratch on it would be repeated on every print of the film. Then the music and narration were combined, or "mixed," in an optical sound track on the film and the titles were added.

To see creatures from my own illustrations take on life and begin to move to lively music would be, it had seemed to me at the beginning, an almost magical experience. However, by the time we had finished working on the film, I realized that its production had very little to do with magic. But now, many months later, when I see Sun, and Moon, and the water creatures alive and enlarged upon a screen, it all seems magical again.

Excerpts from the article which appeared in *The Horn Book Magazine*, December 1971.

On the Rainbow Trail

by Gerald McDermott

I've been on a journey past paper mountains, flying men, foolish spiders, talking trees, and the flaming arrows of the solar fire. It has been a journey of discovery through the bizarre and exotic forms of world mythology. The Rainbow Trail has become a path for my work as an artist.

The riches of myth are usually lost to us in adulthood . . . But myths have a deep appeal and significance for the human mind, and the task of the artist is to reawaken these images. The purpose of my journey has been to explore and share the evocative qualities of these ancient tales with those still open to the message of myth.

Animated films and illustrated books have carried me along this path of exploration. The choice of these media grew out of early experience with several forms of artistic expression. Encouraged and supported by my parents, I attended special classes at the Detroit Institute of Arts from the age of four. Every Saturday, from early childhood through early adolescence, was spent in those halls. I virtually lived in the museum, drawing and painting and coming to know the works of that great collection. I've kept a brush in my hand ever since.

A brief but glorious career as a child radio-actor had its influence. From the age of nine until eleven (that is, until my voice suddenly changed), I was

---

Gerald McDermott was the 1975 winner of the Caldecott Medal for his book, Arrow to the Sun. *As a film-maker as well as illustrator, he has most often made the hero-quest, inspired by myth and legend, the subject matter of his work. His film interpretations communicate on visual, emotional, psychological, and intellectual levels — but even more, they fascinate and entertain all ages.*

heard regularly in a show that specialized in dramatizing folk tales and legends. Working with professional actors and learning how music and sound effects are integrated in a dramatic context were indispensable experiences for a future filmmaker.

And, of course, I was directly influenced by motion pictures, especially those animated epics that evoked a dream world. My view of these changed, however, under the discipline of Bauhaus-based design training at Cass Technical High School. As my ideas and tastes formed, I began to feel sure that the medium of animation could offer more than giggling, white-gloved mice. These interests merged during my college years when I began to experiment with animated films. My principal goal was to design films that were highly stylized in color and form. I also hoped to touch upon themes not dealt with in conventional cartoons. Instinctively, I turned to folklore as a source for thematic material.

The Stonecutter, a Japanese folk tale . . . was my first animated film. It is an ancient fable of a man's foolish longing for power — a tale of wishes and dreams that can be understood on many levels. Its attraction was its elegant simplicity and magical quality. In its structure and symbolism, *The Stonecutter* prefigures my later films: The story contains in microcosm the basic theme of self-transformation that was consciously developed in my later work.

While my approach to the graphic design of *The Stonecutter* was unconventional, traditional animation techniques were used to set the designs in motion. I've continued to utilize these methods because they offer the greatest possible degree of control over the final film. The basic device is the storyboard, a series of about one hundred quick sketches outlining the high points of the action. This serves as a visual script and is referred to continually through the many months of production. Because from four to six thousand drawings are required to animate each of the later films, the storyboard was an essential device in quelling those shape-shifting creatures — design and continuity.

The storyboard is crucial to the second phase of production: the composition and recording of sound-track music. An original musical score has been commissioned for each of my films. The composer studies the storyboard, mood and pacing are discussed, and scene timings are established. The musicians assemble in a studio, and the resulting recording is transferred to sprocketed magnetic tape. This tape is run through a synchronizer, frame by frame, and each note of music is marked on a master timing sheet. We know precisely where each beat falls, and the thousands of final drawings are done to these exact notations. In this way, a perfect synchronization of sound and image movement can be achieved — an effect impossible to obtain if music were added on after the filming was complete.

The bulk of production time is devoted to rendering the thousands of final drawings on paper, acetate, and colored gel. It is obsessive work, at times repetitive and boring, and demands a degree of fanatic devotion — one identifies with the medieval Irish monk illuminating a manuscript in his cell. And budgets for educational films often impose a monk-like austerity.

Once the drawings are finished, they are carefully numbered and noted on the master timing sheets. The cameraman photographs the drawings, one by one, in sequence with the sound track. Finally, after a year of research, planning, recording, drawing, and photographing, the work is complete, and twelve minutes of animation unreels upon the screen. It is an exciting twelve minutes, however. Unlike live-action production — where a mass of footage is shot, viewed, reviewed, edited, and re-edited — the first time I view my film it is complete.

Soon after finishing my first film, I had the immense good fortune to meet Joseph Campbell. Campbell has written extensively and eloquently of the relationships between mythology and modern psychology . . . Campbell has shown that the prime function of mythology is to supply the symbols that carry the human spirit forward, "to waken and give guidance to the energies of life." These ideas, illuminated in Campbell's *The Hero with a Thousand Faces*, became the basis for all my subsequent work.

During the production of *Flight of Icarus*, *Anansi the Spider*, and *The Magic Tree*, I consulted with Campbell on the meanings of the tales that I had chosen to animate. He pointed out that all these mythical stories, even though from cultures as disparate as Japan, ancient Crete, and Africa, share a common theme . . . they deal with the universal idea of the hero quest. Its classic form is delineated by Campbell: "A hero ventures forth from the world of common day into a region of supernatural wonder: fabulous forces are there encountered and a decisive victory is won: the hero comes back from this mysterious adventure with the power to bestow boons on his fellow man."[1]

One can visualize this quest as a circular journey where certain symbols, clothed in the garments of the culture that created the myth, are encountered again and again. Tasaku, the lowly stonecutter, seeks to rise in power through the transforming magic of a mountain spirit; Daedalus and Icarus seek release with magic wings; Mavungu seeks happiness with a magic princess. All journey forth and undergo a series of supernatural events.

Even that loveable rogue, Anansi, goes on a journey. He is a trickster, a comic shadow of the mythic hero. No mystical experience beckons Anansi; he simply "gets lost and falls into trouble." His descent into the abyss consists of being swallowed by a large fish. He has no inner resources with which to save himself; instead, these are divided among six spider sons. His sons do manage to rescue him, but because of this division, the celestial reward of the moon eludes them all.

In each of these films, I was concerned with the circular journey of the individual who sets forth on a quest of self-fulfillment. In psychological terms, he must make a break with the past, overcome obstacles to change, and grow. Ideally, the seeker can then return, his full potential realized, and take his place in society with the "wisdom and power to serve others."

This theme finds its fullest expressions in my book and in my film of *Arrow to the Sun* — with a significant difference. In previous works, the circle was broken. Through some weakness or failing, or perhaps sheer foolishness, the protagonist fails in his search, and the ultimate boon is lost. In this Pueblo Indian tale, however, the circle is complete, and the questing hero successfully finishes his jour-

ney. It is the symbolism of this beautiful myth that I would like to discuss.

Before I do, however, I want to mention one of my personal artistic trials, the transition from film to printed page. This jarring shift from a medium of time to a medium of space posed special problems. When George Nicholson, now Editorial Director of Viking Junior Books, put forth the idea of book adaptations of my African folklore films, it seemed an easy task. After all, four thousand discarded animated drawings were stacked up in my studio. Why not simply shuffle through them, choose forty, and send them off to the printer? Because the result would be a souvenir program of the film — a totally unacceptable solution.

We returned to the original film storyboard, and I tried to reconceive the visual material in a series of double spreads. It was an unsettling experience because the control I enjoyed as a film director was lost. There was no longer a captive audience in a darkened room, its gaze fixed upon hypnotic flickering shadows. Gone were the music and sound effects and the ability to guide the viewer through a flow of images with a carefully planned progression. Now the reader was in control. The reader could begin at the end of the book or linger for ten minutes over a page or perhaps merely glance at half a dozen others. As an artist, I was challenged to resolve these problems.

When I began my work on *Arrow to the Sun*, however, I knew from the outset that the book and the film would be conceived concurrently. With the sensitive and patient collaboration of my editor at Viking, Linda Zuckerman, and my art director, Suzanne Haldane, I sought to solve the problems of continuity and design present in the earlier books. The introduction of large areas of quiet space, filled with solid, rich color, improves the pacing. The use of the Rainbow Trail motif, a multi-colored band, helps to guide the reader's eye across the page. The elimination of text from many spreads allows the images to speak. These are some of the techniques that eased my passage as an artist. Though story line and character design were shared, the book in form, texture, and color took on a life of its own.

In outline and impact, this ancient, pre-Conquest Pueblo Indian tale is a perfect example of the

---

1 Joseph Campbell, *The Hero with a Thousand Faces*, Princeton, New Jersey, Princeton University Press, 1949, p. 30.

classic motif of the hero quest. The hero of this myth, which is the creation of a solar-oriented culture, is a young boy who must seek his true father. The object of his search, the Lord of the Sun, embodies the constancy and power of life-sustaining solar fire — a symbol that is central to Pueblo ritual. The sun, in Carl Jung's phrase, is "the classic symbol of the unity and divinity of self."

Corn, the staff of life for the people of the pueblos, is an important companion symbol to the sun. The constant life-sustaining warmth of the sun nurtures the golden ears of corn. In searching for a graphic motif that would unite these two concepts, I slowly turned an ear of corn in my hands, studying the color, texture, and form. Then I broke the ear in half. At that moment, the symbol hidden beneath the surface was revealed — a moment recreated in my film. The cross section of the ear of corn, with its concentric rings and radiating rays of kernels, forms a perfect image of the sun.

If one looks at the tip of an ear of corn — an important ritual article in Pueblo culture — one sees that four kernels come together to form a quadrilateral sign. I took this flowered cross, with its four kernel rays, and bound it by a solar circle. This became the unifying visual element in my retelling of *Arrow to the Sun*.

It first appears as the spark of life, then as the hero's amulet. It identifies him as he proceeds on his journey through a landscape permeated with the golden hues of sun and corn.

The boy is a child of the divine world and the world of men. He is the offspring of Sky Father and Earth Mother — a lineage he shared with other great heroes of world mythology. "[T]he hero destined to perform miracles . . . can have no earthly father . . . his seed has to be planted by heavenly powers. His mother, however, is earthly, and so he is born both god and man. Always the chosen one unites within himself in this way the two spheres."[2]

His questing path is the Rainbow Trail — a multihued border motif that appears in the sand paintings, pottery designs, and weaving of the Southwest. It runs through the pages of my book as well; down through the sky to the pueblo, across the earth, blazing up to the sun, framing the drama of the kivas, and bursting forth at the moment of the hero's assimilation to the sun.

The Arrowmaker is encountered on the Rainbow Trail. He is a *shaman* — a man of magical powers. Only he has an open eye and the inner vision required to perceive the Boy's true heritage. He provides the supernatural aid that enables the Boy to continue his journey. The magical arrow that he fashions releases the Boy from his earthbound state, just as one of wisdom opens the closed mind of another. He sends the Boy on the self-revealing way of the father-seeking hero.

Upon passing through the fiery sun door, the Boy confronts the mighty Lord of the Sun. This is hardly the completion of the journey, however, but the beginning of the true challenge. Despite its colorful surface and happy conclusion, like similar myths, "its content proper refers to a terrifyingly serious reality: initiation, that is, passing, by way of a symbolic death and resurrection, from ignorance and immaturity to the spiritual age of the adult."[3]

The Boy must descend into the abyss of the ceremonial chambers — the four kivas — to prove his heritage. He must face these tests and emerge reborn from the dark womb of the kiva. A true hero, he accepts the challenge, " 'Father, . . . I will endure these trials.' " Lions, serpents, and bees await the Boy. In the ensuing confrontations, though threatened by these creatures, he is not destroyed. Significantly, neither does he destroy the animals, for they represent the dark forces of our own unconscious. They are the shadow beings of the dream state, the internal demons that torment us and block our growth. We cannot destroy them, but we can calm them and integrate them with our functions. We can assume their positive qualities and put them at our service.

2 Heinrich Zimmer, *The King and the Corpse*, New York, Pantheon Books, Inc., p. 148.

3 Mircea Eliade, *Myth and Reality*, New York, Harper & Row, Publishers, 1963, p. 201.

This interpretation is quite different from the one we might apply to the mythology of the West which is most familiar to us. It represents a kinship and reverence for the natural world that is opposed to Greek and Hebrew tradition. Heracles destroys the titanic snake, the Hydra. He kills the lion, strips it, and wears its skin as a symbol of his dominance. Absolute domination is the message of these myths. But for our Indian hero, the human world and the animal world are reconciled. . . . The Boy assumes the strengths of the lions, even as they become purring kittens at his feet. He overcomes the squirming chaos of the serpents and and creates a circle, a symbol of wholeness and unity as is the corn-sustaining sun. (The serpents inhabit the maizefield, and devour the corn-destroying rodents.) The bees, which can sting with killing power, instead give the miracle gift of sun-colored honey to the boy.

The deepest point of the descent into the abyss occurs in the Kiva of Lightning. Here flashes the polar opposite of the constant warmth of the sun. Unpredictable and violent, it shatters the immature form of the Boy. When he emerges from this final crisis, he is reborn and "filled with the power of the sun" — filled with a spiritual awareness born of his trials. If this solar symbolism seems remote, perhaps we should listen to the response of a nine-year-old to *Arrow to the Sun*: "I think that the Lord of the Sun knew all along who the Boy really was, but he made the Boy go through the tests anyway, so that the Boy would know who he was.'"

The journey on the Rainbow Trail is near its end. The Boy, radiant in his new garments, returns to earth bearing the message of his father. He began as an individual searching for his true identity, isolated from his community. He completes the journey as a self-aware messenger of life-sustaining powers, ready to take his place in the community. As Joseph Campbell has observed, "The ultimate aim of the quest, if one is to return, must be . . . the wisdom and power to serve others." Surrounded by the people of his village, joined with the Corn Maiden, watched over by Sky Father and Earth Mother, enclosed within the arc of the Rainbow Trail, the hero steps onto the World Center and joins in the Dance of Life.

The Rainbow Trail of the artist has come full circle. It is not an end, but a continuation, an ever-repeated cycle. The challenge is eternal: to descend again and again into the "image-producing abyss" to discover visual evocations of the compelling myths of mankind.

Excerpts from the article which appeared in *The Horn Book Magazine*, April 1975.

142

Articles, Books, and Catalogs

suggested for Reading and Reference

Alderson, Brian. *Looking at Picture Books 1973*. Catalog of an exhibition prepared by Brian Alderson, arranged by The National Book League (England). Distributed in the United States by the Children's Book Council, 67 Irving Place, New York, New York 10003.

Bader, Barbara. *American Picturebooks from Noah's Ark to The Beast Within*. New York: Macmillan Publishing Co., Inc./London: Collier Macmillan Publishers, 1976.

Cannon, Rupert Vernon, and Wallis, F. G. *Graphic reproduction; copy preparation and process*. London: Vista Books, 1963.

Chappell, Warren. *The Living Alphabet*. Charlottesville, The University Press of Virginia, 1975.

Chappell, Warren. *A Short History of the Printed Word*. New York, Alfred A. Knopf, Inc., 1970.

Colby, Jean Poindexter. *Writing, Illustrating and Editing Children's Books*. New York: Hastings House, Publishers, Inc., 1970.

Ede, Charles, ed. *The Art of the Book; some record of work carried out in Europe and the USA, 1939-1950*. London/New York: Studio Publications, 1951.

Giorgiou, Constantine. *Children and Their Literature*. Englewood Cliffs, N. J.: Prentice-Hall, Inc., 1969.

Gill, Bob and Lewis, John. *Illustration: aspects and directions*. New York: Reinhold Publishing Corp., 1964.

Graphis. "International Survey of Children's Book Illustration." Zurich: Walter Herdeg, The Graphis Press, July 1975, No. 177.

Hale, Nancy. *Mary Cassatt*. Garden City, N. Y.: Doubleday & Company, 1975.

Hürlimann, Bettina. *Picture-Book World*. translated and edited by Brian W. Alderson. New York: The World Publishing Company, 1968.

Jacques, Robin. *Illustrators at work*. London: Studio Books, 1963.

Jones, Helen L. *Robert Lawson, Illustrator, A Selection of His Characteristic Illustrations*. Boston/Toronto: Little, Brown and Company, 1972.

Kingman, Lee, ed. *Newbery and Caldecott Medal Books: 1956-1965*. Boston: The Horn Book, Inc., 1965.

Kingman, Lee, ed. *Newbery and Caldecott Medal Books: 1966-1975*. Boston: The Horn Book, Inc., 1975.

Kingman, Lee; Foster, Joanna; and Lontoft, Ruth Giles, eds. *Illustrators of Children's Books: 1957-1966*. Boston: The Horn Book, Inc., 1968.

Klemin, Diana. *The Art of Art for Children's Books*. New York: Clarkson N. Potter, 1966.

Klemin, Diana. *The Illustrated Book*. New York; Clarkson N. Potter, 1970.

Lamb, Lynton. *Drawing for Illustration*. London/New York: Oxford University Press, 1962.

Lanes, Selma G. *Down the Rabbit Hole*. New York: Atheneum Publishers, 1961.

Larkin, David, editor. *The Art of Nancy Ekholm Burkert*. Introduced by Michael Danoff. New York, Harper & Row, Publishers, 1977.

Lewis, John Noel Claude. *The Twentieth Century Book, Its Illustration and Design*. London: Studio Vista/New York, Reinhold, 1967.

Lorraine, Walter. "On Illustrators — My View." *The Calendar*, New York: Children's Book Council, Vol. xxxiv. No. 1. March-August 1975.

MacCann, Donnarae and Richard, Olga. *The Child's First Books. A Critical Study of Pictures and Texts*. New York: The H. W. Wilson Company, 1973.

Mahony, Bertha E.; Latimer, Louise P.; and Folmsbee, Beulah, eds. *Illustrators of Children's Books: 1744-1945*. Boston: The Horn Book, Inc., 1947.

Miller, Bertha Mahony and Field, Elinor Whitney, eds. *Caldecott Medal Books: 1938-1957*. Boston: The Horn Book, Inc., 1957.

Miller, Bertha Mahony; Viguers, Ruth Hill; and Dalphin, Marcia, eds. *Illustrators of Children's Books: 1946-1956*. Boston: The Horn Book, Inc. 1958.

Muir, Percy. *English Children's Books 1600-1900*. London: B. T. Batsford, Ltd., 1954.

Pennell, Joseph. *The Illustration of Books; a manual for the use of students, notes for a course of lectures at the Slade School, University College*. Ann Arbor, Michigan: Gryphon Books, 1971.

Pitz, Henry C. *A Treasury of American Book Illustration*. New York/London: American Studio Books, Watson-Guptill Publications, Inc., 1947.

Pitz, Henry C. *Howard Pyle.* New York: Clarkson N. Potter, Inc., 1975.

Pitz, Henry C. *Illustrating Children's Books: history, technique, production.* New York: Watson-Guptill Publications, 1963.

Pitz, Henry C. *The Brandywine Tradition.* Boston: Houghton Mifflin Company, 1969.

Ross, Eulalie Steinmetz. *The Spirited Life, Bertha Mahony Miller and Children's Books.* Boston: The Horn Book, Inc., 1973.

Ryder, John. *Artists of a Certain Line. A Selection of Illustrators for Children's Books.* London: The Bodley Head, 1960.

Slythe, R. Margaret. *The Art of Illustration, 1750-1900.* London: Library Association, 1970.

Spurrier, Steven. *Black and White Illustration.* New York: Pitman, 1954.

Stone, Bernard and Eckstein, Arthur. *Preparing Art for Printing.* New York: Reinhold, 1965.

Yolen, Jane. *Writing Books for Children.* Boston: The Writer, Inc., 1974.

Index

146